MAKE
LOVE
YOUR
AIM

BOOKS BY EUGENIA PRICE . . .

Share My Pleasant Stones
Never a Dull Moment
Early Will I Seek Thee
The Burden Is Light
What Is God Like?
Beloved World
A Woman's Choice
Find Out for Yourself
God Speaks to Women Today
Woman to Woman
Just As I Am
The Wider Place
Make Love Your Aim
The Unique World of Women
Learning to Live From the Gospel
The Beloved Invader
New Moon Rising
Lighthouse
No Pat Answers
Discoveries — Made From Living My New Life
Learning to Live From the Acts
Don Juan McQueen

Eugenia Price

MAKE LOVE YOUR AIM

ZONDERVAN PUBLISHING HOUSE
OF THE ZONDERVAN CORPORATION
GRAND RAPIDS, MICHIGAN 49506

MAKE LOVE YOUR AIM

Copyright © 1967 by Eugenia Price

Seventeenth printing   1976

Scripture quotations are from the Revised Standard Version of the Bible copyrighted 1946 and 1952 by the Division of Christian Education, National Council of Churches in the United States of America, and used by permission. Grateful appreciation is also expressed to: Farrar, Straus and Giroux, New York, N.Y. for permission to quote from *The Ability To Love* by Allan Fromme (copyright 1963, 1965). To John Knox Press for permission to quote from *The Gospel According to Peanuts,* by Robert L. Short, © M. E. Bratcher 1965. To Zondervan Publishing House for permission to quote from *Congo Crisis,* by Joseph T. Bayly. © 1966 Zondervan Publishing House.

Library of Congress Catalog Card Number 67-22686
Printed in the United States of America

To my friend,
Floyd Thatcher

"An aim in life is the only fortune worth finding."

Robert Louis Stevenson

CONTENTS

I.

II.

III.

PREFACE

After the unusual experience of writing *The Wider Place,* (Zondervan, 1966) I began to be aware that I had explored only one side of the coin of *freedom* which God offers to everyone who wants it enough to enter in. My own capacities were stretched in the writing, and the direct relationship of freedom to love gripped me. I felt I had only begun the exploration, and my feeling was verified when (unknown to each other) my editor, Mr. Floyd Thatcher, and my friend, Dr. Anna Mow made identical suggestions to me for a book to follow *The Wider Place* — a book on love.

Their suggestions confirmed what I had begun to realize: There is no freedom without love and no love without freedom. Love and freedom are two sides of the same coin — neither fully explorable by a mere mortal, but both of a piece. And both outright gifts from God.

Love and Freedom are gifts from God, but *Make Love Your Aim* has to do with our part in learning how to make use of these gifts.

We can study the nature of love for all the years of our earthly lives and still not plumb its depths. Yet, the merest child can grasp love's essence, can learn to make use of it. The merest child *can* do this, but most adults have never given love an honest try. Love is the aim of the few. If it could become the aim of the many, our world would be changed. Making love our aim is quite simply, giving God the freedom to act as *he* would act. We do not learn how to give God this freedom in a minute, even when we have decided to make love the aim of our life. Loving requires practice, and one intent of this book is to emphasize the necessity for the practice of love. We tend to pray: "Oh, God, give me more of your love." He has already given all of his love when he gave himself: God is love. Our part is to permit love to become a habit by practicing all that we see of it in our human relationships. It is a gift, but we must form the habit of using the gift or it lies worthless in the drawer of our inertia.

I feel it necessary to explain once more that what I have written in this book, as in others, is written for persons with basically normal minds. When I speak of showing love in these pages, it is *always* with the thought in mind that when a mentally unbalanced person is involved, we can frequently do more damage than good. Increasingly, from sometimes bitter experience, I urge professional counsel in these instances.

If it appears (and it will to some) that I have referred often to the matter of the need for love between the races, it is because I am genuinely troubled by the racial barriers which still stand high within the Christian church. These barriers are usually invisible, but too often they still stand. I propagate no cause here, except the cause of Christ who commanded that we are to love one another as he loved us. With Jesus Christ, the Saviour of all mankind, there are no barriers.

More than ever before I am indebted to Joyce Blackburn for expert correction of my manuscript; to my mother, who goes on being my constant source of encouragement; to Frances Pitts and Anna Mow for helpfully critical readings and once again deep thanks to Elsie Goodwillie for her careful and loving handling of the typescript.

And not for duty's sake, but for love's sake, I feel compelled to thank the Father for being love and for revealing himself so plainly in Jesus Christ that no one ever *needs* to doubt his heart.

EUGENIA PRICE

St. Simons Island, Georgia

Part I

". . . for God is love." I John 4:8 (RSV)

> Man comes to know God is love
> when he comes to know
> that God *is* as he revealed himself
> in Jesus Christ.

Chapter 1

God Is Still Love

IN THE DEEPEST HEART of every man God planted a longing for himself, *as he is*: a God of love. No matter what we say, our hearts cry out for God to care, to be involved with us, to love us. This is his idea. He created this longing in us. It is the longing toward the "light that lighteth every man who cometh into the world."

The human race longs for love because the human race longs for God. God and love are not similar. Love is not merely one of God's characteristics. "God *is* love."

No matter how it looks to us, nothing changes this. He is not dead. He *is*. And if we believe he is, then we can know that he is love.

Anyone can be freed to see both the truth about our world and the truth about God and come out free not only to believe in love, but to love. This does not happen overnight, but it can begin happening at any moment to anyone, and because God is growth and life as well as love, it can go on happening. Light from

God does not dim, as light from the sun dims at the end of a day. Light from God grows clearer, and only appears to dim as we insist upon standing in the shadows made by our human tendency to remain stunted. A baby bird in a nest, who refuses to try his wings, stays nest-bound, stunted in body and courage and daring, eventually dies. It feels safe in the nest, but that kind of safety is intended to last only for a short period. The time comes to fly, and those who fear or refuse flight enter the realm of death. We can peer fearfully over the side of our personal nests and see only the distance we could fall. We can also peer over the side of our nests and, making use of continuing knowledge of God, dare to fly—facing both the fact of the danger and the fact of God's ability to sustain us. The stunted, confused, or pompous among us always questions this.

The *stunted* mind looks at the ugly facts — the brutality in our streets, the mass slaughter from falling bombs, murder at the hands of mentally deranged individuals, the senseless deaths on our highways and from still unconquered disease — and blames God. The stunted mind looks at only one set of facts — the ugly facts about the world around us—and draws back, never examining the facts about God, the fact of God.

The *confused* mind tends to fly in all directions at once, with no destination and no sense of distance. Looking only at the turmoil and heartache and tragedy in our world, the confused mind is unable to focus on anything. Happiness is too short-lived to hold the attention. Tragedy and violence too terrible. Failure too complete, fear too smothering. Looking at the chaos in the world can lead only to confusion, because nothing holds the gaze. The confused mind must dart from fear and brutality and grief and failure to something else just for relief. There is only one stable, reliable, eternal focal point — the fact of God himself, and the confused mind, the mind unsure about His nature, cannot concentrate on Him long enough or steadily enough to learn.

The *pompous* mind demands that God live up to its idea of what he should be like, if it admits his existence at all. God cannot be a God of love to the pompous mind because he permits suffering and death. (I understand this mind. I once possessed it. Looking at the carnage of Hiroshima I decided God did not exist at all. I preferred that he be nonexistent rather than capable of allowing such agony.)

Since the pompous mind forms omniscient concepts about everything, so it must form its own concept of love, but until it understands something of the true nature of love it is only understood in the true nature of God. It either declares him nonexistent, or declares him to be a fiend.

But how does man come to know that God is love? That love is because God is? That the love of God is not only available for any man to experience, it is available for any man to demonstrate? How do we come to know the true nature of love? By reading a book or embracing a particular philosophy or doctrine? Do we learn love from the Bible? From other human beings who expound it? Do we learn about the nature of love by practice? Is it an emotional or a spiritual exercise?

It is all of these to lesser and greater degrees, but it is more. And it is the intention of this book to share some insights into *how* — not only to learn of God's love, but to make this very love the aim of life.

Man comes to know that God is love when he comes to know that *God is* as he revealed himself in Jesus Christ. The utter child-like simplicity of this truth is often distorted (by the stunted, the confused, or the pompous mind) into over-simplification. Over-simplification and childlike simplicity are not the same. It is an over-simplification to claim that God backs us up whatever our point of view, our pet theory. It seems sometimes, as we listen to political speeches, read editorials, current novels, essays and even religious books, that almost everyone is using God in this way. The extreme liberal (labels have become over-simplifications too) attempts to imitate the earthly life of Jesus Christ by giving himself to the cause of his choice and ends up substituting his cause and his own sacrificial efforts in its behalf for God himself. The extreme conservative does the same thing with different words. God, to the scripture shouting racist or Federal Government hater, is always on his side. According to him, God thought up segregation in the first place. He can give you verse and chapter to prove God prefers white Anglo-Saxons. With the same authority, the extreme liberal looks down his nose at anyone who does not follow what he believes to be the example of Christ into whatever street demonstration involves him at the moment.

The extreme conservative is at once stunted, confused and pompous. The extreme liberal is at once stunted, confused and pompous. God is not involved in our extremes. He is God. And he is love. The kind of love which never takes sides except its own. God has always been and will always be on the side of love. He could not be any other way because he cannot change his own nature and still be God. *Extremism* binds. *Love* frees. *Extremism* divides. *Love* makes us one. Love cannot be extreme because it has, if it is authentic, the very balance of God at its center.

If God is all balance, all integrating (in the sense that he is making us whole), all inclusive — his love embracing the irritating among us who revel in extremes — then how is it that extremists can hide behind him as it were? Can use him to justify their intolerance and bigotry and rigidity?

The answer to this question is not at all complex. It is we who complicate it. The answer is simple — so simple it insults our intellectual arrogance. It has directly to do with the purpose of this book. It has directly to do with our pursuit of freedom. It has directly to do with the contradictory pictures we get of our world's dilemma because it has directly to do with man's frightening common failure to understand what real love is all about.

The man or woman who uses God to back up his or her own favorite doctrine or cause is doing just that — using God. This form of blasphemy is being practiced every hour of every day by all of us in some form or other. Even the atheistic Communist uses his lack of belief in God as a plank for his political platform. He is using God. The frightened, frantic "preserver of the races" who quotes scripture to "prove" that God meant white people to be superior and keep those of other races "in their place," is using God. As is the the bearded Civil Rights worker who blocks traffic by kneeling to pray in the rush hour at a busy intersection. As is the possessive parent who keeps the lives of grown children in a vise by intimating that if they don't do as they're told they are somehow anti-Christian.

The list is long. The reason for all such spiritual deviations is clear: Love is not involved in any habitual *use* of God. Just as love is never involved in any habitual *use* of another human being. The screaming racist, who lures his followers to violence by "using" their superficial knowledge of God as he quotes scripture to inflame them against their brothers of another color, is "using" his followers just as surely as the possessive parent uses the child to nurture his parental ego.

Love does not *misuse* another. And there is just as much difference in the way God *uses* people to advance the cause of love and the way man *uses* God to advance his own cause as there is difference between God and man.

Any self-centered use man makes of God is misuse. Any use God makes of man is the foundation of his love, *active* redemption.

At the vulnerable heart of God is love. The universal ignorance of love is at the heart of our universal dilemma. *We* have decided, according to our concepts, our own needs, our limited experience, what real love is. And we are, most of us, as far wrong as possible.

It is the purpose of the following chapters to attempt some authentic practical understanding of love itself as it is demonstrated in God.

Any other knowledge of love is half-knowledge, marginal, inelastic, prone to the disease of self-protection, tending toward death. Because only in him (in God) is "life."

And God is still all love.

> . . . real love is giving love
> and remains in
> active motion toward another.

Chapter 2

What Is Love?

LOVE IS THE OTHER side of freedom. There cannot be one without the other. Freedom is a popular pursuit these days, as it has been in the past, but is it freedom we seek or are we in reality seeking love? Love must be at hand before freedom can be found.

We childishly dream of a state of lessening responsibilities and an absence of restrictions. But the child who is never curbed, never disciplined, rebels rightly against a lack of love from his parents. Because love involves discipline and responsibility.

Freedom of speech is *not* the right to say abusive and destructive things about one's enemies. Freedom of worship does not mean ignoring God. Freedom from want does not provide an excuse to "go on relief." Freedom from fear does not relieve one of responsibility to face danger with courage.

Freedom is truth in action, and for the Christian it is simply God in action. Is this what love is?

What is love *not?*

It is not necessarily *eloquence*. It may be. We all tend to feel that love eloquently expressed is somehow deeper. But this is not always so.

> Though I speak with the tongues of men and of angels, but have not love, I am a noisy gong or a clanging cymbal.

Paul was an eloquent man, an intellectually learned man, one of the most gifted writers in all literature, but he saw through eloquence to love.

Love is not necessarily wisdom, as the world recognizes wisdom and learning:

> And if I have prophetic powers and understand all mysteries and all knowledge . . . but I have not love, I am nothing.

Love is not necessarily faith:

> . . . and if I have all faith, so as to remove mountains, but have not love, I am nothing.

We are often misled here, but love is not necessarily self-sacrifice and generosity, either:

> If I give away all I have, and if I deliver my body to be burned, but have not love, I gain nothing.

Our human tendency is to measure love by its eloquence — the beauty of its expression, how romantic or how elevated it makes us *feel*. But this is not the essence of love. We likewise measure and appraise love by knowledge and understanding: We expect the educated class of people to know how to show more love to their offspring, to have more understanding of the psychology of the young mind and to be therefore more sensitive, more able to cope with problems. But this is not always true. In fact, it is too frequently untrue. The children of Better-suburbia go right on startling us with their rebellious conduct, their contempt of parental authority — of any authority. Educated wives seem not to love their educated husbands more than the dull-faced, illiterate mountain woman, old before her time, loves her equally limited husband with whom she has shared work and more work through the years of their lives together.

Even faith is not necessarily a part of love. It can, the same as eloquence and knowledge, exist alone — aside from love. A famous baseball pitcher once gave an interview in which he witnessed glowingly to his faith — a faith no one doubted. But when he discovered that the interview was to be used on a program sponsored by a denomination of which he did not approve, he cancelled it. His faith seemed apart from love. Some men and women live by the faith they have in the Bible, and it is a real faith, but they live excluding those who do not agree with their interpretation of the Bible they believe in. Interpretations do not need love. People do.

Love cannot always be measured by self-sacrifice or generosity either. One of the most selfish, sharp-spoken, difficult women I have ever known sacrificed not only her time but her health in order to put her son through the long, expensive education required for his profession. But she did not love him enough to accept the wife he married. A man whose excessive gener-

osity with other people left his wife with nothing but
debts at his death, shunned the responsibility of love.
Men and women give their bodies to be burned or shot
or crucified for a faith that may spread destruction
instead of love. Men give themselves to be shot on
both sides of every war — and where is the result as
measured in love?

All of these things: eloquence, knowledge, faith,
generosity, self-sacrifice are an integral part of God's
love, but somehow *in man* they can be separated from
the substance of love itself. It is as though what was
originally whole, intact in the heart of the Father,
somehow comes apart, splits up, separates, becomes
idolatrous when funneled through the complex, fallen
natures of men and women.

Lacking love, we become proud of our eloquence,
proud of our knowledge, proud of our faith; we boast
of our generosity, our self-sacrifice, and the essence
of love, as it is demonstrated by God through his son,
Jesus Christ, is no longer recognizable.

The love of God *is* eloquent, knowledgeable, full of
faith and generosity and self-sacrifice, but Paul believed that we mortals could possess any or all of these
characteristics to an exalted degree and still have no
love.

Do you believe this? Do I? Do we, because we somehow do not agree with Paul in our hearts, tend to
diminish the impact of the love of God by splitting off
his love into the same useless, futile segments into
which we split our own concept of love? Do we diminish God by trying to compress him into our own image so that for us, the true nature of his love is dis-

torted? Depleted? Distorted and depleted by our own feeble attempts at love? Do we so misunderstand what love really is that we misunderstand God himself?

What good is eloquence if impatience is its partner? If unkindness turns it into sophisticated sarcasm to wound and denegate? What good is knowledge if it is patronizing and boastful? What good is faith if it insists on its own way, its own rightness, and causes resentment and irritation? What good is self-sacrifice if it turns to self-pity from lack of recognition, or if it rejoices at wrong? How far from the true nature of love was the woman who sacrificed herself to educate her son when the most she gained was to gloat when her daughter-in-law grew jealous of her?

What — that is creative — could ever come from eloquence or knowledge or faith or self-sacrifice or generosity if one's patience is exhausted in the process?

Paul says:

> Love is patient and kind; love is not jealous or boastful; it is not arrogant or rude. Love does not insist on its own way; it is not irritable or resentful; it does not rejoice at wrong but rejoices in the right. *Love bears all things, believes all things, hopes all things, endures all things.*

These are not new ideas. They are from the beautifully written Love Chapter in Paul's first letter to the people at Corinth. Like many others, I was familiar with the poetry of it, the elevating thought of it, long before I became a Christian. But, if this is all so appealing to us by nature, why is it that we go right on being untouched by it? Why do we go right on acting as though our particular concept of love is even close to the concept of God himself?

Perhaps the answer is as simple as this: We haven't stopped to *think*. We grab onto one or two characteristics which we consider related to love and miss the dynamism, the force — the phenomenon itself. Because to us love *is* a phenomenon. It need not be; it should not be, but it is. So few of us have learned anything of the true nature of love, it remains exceptional — a rarity.

Sometimes we substitute a concept of freedom for love. We watch ourselves and our neighbors and other members of our society struggle for freedom while we omit love. We forget they are two sides of the same coin. The one coin of the realm of God which man must possess if he is to live creatively, redemptively on this earth. Love and freedom are also a key to understanding God. The key to understanding each other. The key to the full life, the key that unlocks the door of all bondage known to man.

I see no way to differentiate between love and freedom. Freedom is the result of love in action. Love is the ultimate goal of freedom. And yet all real freedom begins in love. Love frees. Real love always leaves the loved one free to be himself, herself. His best self. Her best self. Love never restricts, never binds. Love always rejoices in the growth and forward step of the loved one. Freedom is not only the *result* of love in action, it *is* love in action. When a man is set free from his sin, the whole forward movement had to begin in love. The love of God.

For God so loved the world that he *gave*. . . .

Love always gives. It knows how to receive gracefully, but even then it is *giving* joy to the giver. We all know otherwise good people, lovable people, who simply will not permit us to do anything for *them*. They seem happy only when they are giving to us. Jesus was buried in a borrowed tomb, and the very purity of his heart turned his ability to receive into giving. Doesn't he promise us the same ability?

> But as many as received him, to them gave he power to become the sons of God. . . .

We cannot keep to ourselves the love we receive from him; real love is giving love and remains in active motion toward another. Real love gives freedom to the loved one because it concerns itself first of all with the well-being of someone else and never with how that "someone else" is making the lover feel. We show love, true love, when we concern ourselves first and always with the way the other person feels — not with how that other person is making us feel.

Real love frees the loved one, but it also frees the lover. If I love, if you love, we are *free*. We are free because our reactions to a set of circumstances are never, never dependent upon the circumstances themselves. We are not free if our state of mind is determined by what someone else does to us or leaves undone. Those who love are free because their reactions are determined by what *they are*. We become hopeless unless we are convinced once and for all that we cannot love, as God would have us love, without his love being operative in us. *We are* what we come to see about God himself!

No one can define love without defining God. No one can explain love without explaining God. And God can only be defined or explained in Jesus Christ. We cannot enter into a state of being or a realm of conviction if we are ignorant of its source. We cannot grow in the Christian life if we are ignorant of the Christ.

What is love? Love is God, because God is love. If that sounds glib, think about it. It can become the great clarification: We can only learn of love as we learn of God. Jesus said, ". . . learn of me."

There is no other way to learn of love.

> God is love and love is
> man's deepest need . . .
> When man meets God,
> man's deepest need is met.

Chapter 3

Who Needs Love?

GOD HAS ALWAYS BEEN and will always be concerned, first of all with our need.

Children are taught that man was created to ". . . glorify God and enjoy Him forever." This can only sound remote and ultra-mystical to a citizen of the twentieth century, who has never stopped to think that God, himself, embodies the basic need of every human being. God *is* love and love is man's deepest need, and therefore when man meets God, man's deepest need is met.

This is true, but our complex minds cannot, without a struggle, accept its simplicity. This complexity of man involves God's risk in having created us with free wills. He must likewise risk our complexity. A complexity he also created. It can never be said that God made it easy for himself. Man, as a thinking, emotional being, cannot be simple. If he were, he could not cope with the scientific problems of the universe — macrocosm or microcosm. If man were a simple being, he could never cope with the education of the young, the legislation of laws — their enforcement. Man is God's highest, most complex, most productive, most puzzling creation, and to attempt to oversimplify him is sheer insanity.

And yet, at the center of faith lies the ability to accept without question the fact of a loving God. A God who, by being love, can meet man's deepest need.

For now, we will *be* childlike enough to accept this great simplification. In the last chapter of this book an attempt will be made to see something of *how* this kind of unquestioning acceptance can become possible for us, even the most doubting among us. But for the moment, recognizing that God *does* meet man's deepest need, the need for love, as we go beyond the generalization that everyone needs love, and look at some of the particular needs for it among certain types of people.

No one questions a child's need of love. Verified cases of homeless babes having been loved or ignored in hospitals during infancy, prove without doubt that for normal emotional, mental and physical growth, babies require loving care and affection. But children must be loved into loving. Apparently we are born with only the capacity to love. A capacity that can be trained or conditioned to respond to the love of another. The mother, by her mother-talk, her hourly watchful care for the infant's needs, by her show of affection, loves the child into loving her. One day the baby smiles at her, reaches toward her, begins to respond to her love.

It is a high moment for a mother, who should undoubtedly be able to know something of the joy in God's heart when an unresponsive human heart shows its first response to him.

But a baby's need for love is one-sided. Its need is to receive love. Until the child has been loved into loving in return, the entire procedure is for it to receive.

And here is the crux of the failure of adults to understand or to practice love. When we think of our need for love, too often we think only in terms of how much we need someone else to love us — as though we were still babies. We dwell on our need to be appreciated, respected, pampered a little, thanked. We think of how much we would enjoy the attention of other human beings. And here the great distortion occurs. We are just as much in need of giving love to someone else as we are of receiving it. Perhaps more so. I have wondered about this as the years slip past me. Before I was forty I expected love, love turned toward *me*. I was happy or unhappy according to how much I received of what I wanted and felt my due. Now, I am beginning to see that what really fulfills me, what seems to be truly my native air is — to love. And to love means to make free. The greatest gift anyone can offer a loved one is freedom. Here again, we are given a glimpse into the calibre of God's love. He never pushes or forces his attentions or his will upon us. He not only created us free, he leaves us free. And God does this because he knows, as no one else can ever know, that anything done for duty's sake is not done for love's sake. If you attend church or read your Bible or pray at night because you feel it to be your duty to God, you are missing exactly half of what a love relationship with him has to offer. The quality of *his* love never varies. He doesn't give to us because it is *his* duty to do so. He gives because he loves. His half of the experience of love we cannot corrupt or diminish. But if we are serving him or worshipping him from a sense of duty, we miss that other half — our half, that can make the perfect whole. That other half that makes up the "perfect love" which casts out fear.

We will never have a way of finding out, but I would not be surprised (if we had a way) to learn that almost everyone in the world who feels unloved or lonely or rejected has failed in some way to love God for love's sake. He has created us so that our involvement is as important as his involvement. God is always actively moving toward us. His involvement with us is as complete as his commitment to us. But we tend either to attempt to return this love of his by service for duty's sake or by the equally stultifying practice of worrying and fussing over our own righteousness or lack of it. Some persons overwork in what they call God's behalf and others over-analyze their spiritual states. Both miss the point of the free, creative exchange of love which God intends.

We all need love. But we all need to *give* love more that we need to sit back and receive it.

Parents need to receive love from their children. Most of them deserve it. But if the "love" they claim to feel for their offspring binds and forces them to duty, the parents are missing half of what God has for them. If we cause anyone to feel compelled to do this or that for us so that we won't feel neglected or rejected, we are cutting off, not only our loved ones, but ourselves from the all-freeing, all-redemptive act of participating love. "My children wouldn't think of letting us spend our anniversary alone. Why, do you know my son and his wife flew all the way from the west coast to New England to be with us on our forty-fifth wedding anniversary? Yep, that's what they did. My son missed out on a good business deal to do it, too. I could tell he was fidgety all the while they were here, but they put their parents first, believe you me."

The old man gloated happily, but he missed the point of love entirely. More than that, he further bound his son *and* his son's apparently docile wife more deeply into a duty relationship.

If we *want* to go to Grandma's house for Christmas every year, that's great. If our hearts direct the journey, it can be one of joy. If duty forces it, the very heart of Christmas, which is *giving love*, drops out. When love has to be measured by a visit on a certain date each year, it is no more reliable than the weather.

"Let's stay at a motel, Daddy. We're all so tired. You'll be tired when you go back to the office if we spend the night at Aunt Mary's. She doesn't have enough beds." But Aunt Mary wouldn't "understand." The scene is repeated everywhere in our world every day more times than anyone could count. Aunt Mary needs love too. But it is possible the Aunt Marys of the world would receive more love if they could catch on to the fact that sometimes people don't feel up to being "entertained." Sometimes they just want to be alone and sleep.

Clergymen need love. They are expected to give it day in and day out, night in and night out to the members of their churches, whether they feel like it or not. But few parishioners love their pastor enough not to be insulted if he is just too weary or too busy to visit them in person and sends his assistant instead.

Employers need love. Even the difficult ones. Particularly the difficult ones. And I am aware that because I happen to earn my living without a boss, I am treading on unfamiliar territory. Still, the territory of love is the territory of God, and God loves even the cruel, seemingly unfeeling variety of business executive who finds it easy to give to charitable organizations which permit tax deductions, but difficult to pay a full salary to a long-time employee who is ill.

"He only pays me 75c an hour and just last week he decided the $3.00 a week I was paying on my charge account wasn't enough, so be began taking out $5.00 from my check!" The mistreated employee wanted to "let him have it." Instead, she baked a cake for his little boy's birthday. This may not change her boss at all, but at least she participated in love with God toward him.

Friends need love from friends. But how many of us love our friends for what they are, embracing faults, failures and selfish streaks and not for *how* they make us feel? Not for the quality of their response to us? "She's just as good as gold when everything is going to suit her. But when something goes wrong, I'm the one who has to hear it all in detail. And if I don't stop what I'm doing and listen just the instant she wants to tell me, she's miffed. Shouldn't a friend be able to understand if I ask her to let me call her back now and then? Shouldn't she care that I may be worried or busy when she gets the urge to call me on the telephone?" Yes, she should. Friends who participate in both sides of love, the human and the divine, not only practice courtesy with each other, they *feel* courteous. A friend who *loves* — even a casual friend or a business acquaintance — will ask if this is a good or bad time for a conversation before launching. Love *breeds sensitivity, not touchiness*. And there is a wide difference.

The bereaved need love. Oh, how they need it! But it is love they need, not platitudes and sermons on eternal life. There are times when *giving love* is merely present in silence, in saying nothing, in doing nothing. Merely in being there, sharing. Before Jesus raised Lazarus, the beloved brother of his friends, Mary and Martha, from the dead, he first was with them, weeping. Love joins, it never sets apart. He did not preach to them about keeping their chins up. He wept with them. He entered in as one of them. He participated in God-love.

"It gets almost funny sometimes," a widow wrote. "My friends really seem to try to help me, but invariably they call and say: 'My husband is out of town tonight, how about dinner with me?' I know I'm the odd one now, but how can I convince them that their kindness is misplaced?" She can't probably. People who "work in" their kindnesses for duty's sake simply have not learned how to participate in love. Have not learned the art of entering in.

Who needs love?

Everyone.

But everyone needs to give love as well as to receive it. Jesus went further when he declared:

It is more blessed to give than to receive.

This is true, not as a spiritual discipline, but as a fact of God himself. Our human love approaches God-love more nearly when it gives. Because God's love is always reaching out, offering itself completely to his loved ones.

And God's loved ones are everyone, everywhere.

Part II

"Make love your aim . . ." I Corinthians 14:1 (RSV)

*Love frees. And freedom incites
experiment and experiment opens wide
the door to creative living.*

Chapter 4

The Freedom of Love

THERE CAN BE NO REAL freedom without
love. There can be the wild-swinging ego on the
loose, the headstrong, opinionated crash program to
get one's own way. There can be license (freedom
abused), but real freedom comes only with the experience and practice of authentic love.

Real freedom survives only in the atmosphere of
giving love.

Jesus said that it is more blessed to give than it is
to receive. In context, he referred to material giving
and material receiving. In depth, (always his words
involved layer upon layer of deeper content) he included in this truth the added blessedness inherent in giving love over receiving it. Those who live by the law
of giving-love are blessed even beyond those who
receive their love.

In all things, it is more blessed to give than to
receive.

But in order to examine the tremendous potential
of the freedom of love, we will look first at the freeing

37

power of love upon the life of the loved one. We mistake and distort what we consider love to such an extent that only by being definite—only by observing the end results of selfish love—can we see clearly how much difference real love can make in a human life.

Repeatedly, I have written of the creative liberty I have been given in my own life through the freeing love offered me for all my years by my mother. By my father too, when he was alive. I must have often perplexed them both during the years in which I was not a Christian. I am sure they knew genuine anxiety over me some of the time. But always, their love came toward me, reminding me of their faith in me, of their generosity, of their expectations for me. I was never permitted to stop believing in myself. To this day, I am convinced that their love, the quality of their love, ultimately did this for me. My own belief in myself bent often and broke once or twice. Theirs never wavered. As with every family, mine had its share of good times and bad times. Not once, through either, did they try to force their problems upon me by insisting (as they had every right to do because they supported me much of the time) that I "come home" in order to make things easier for them for one reason or another. They believed in me and believed that I would make my goal of becoming a professional writer more quickly in a big city, so through any vicissitude of theirs, I was left free.

The results in my life were slow to appear. I still marvel at their patience. But one example of how their unselfish, freeing love got through to me at perhaps the most self-centered period of my life shows the creative effect of their love on me in a rather concrete way. It may sound unimpressive. It may seem what any ordinarily considerate daughter would have done anyway. Not this one. At a time when my career was just beginning to focus my mother fell ill and required serious surgery. It was putting definite financial pressure upon them to keep me in Chicago in my own apartment. Mother needed me with her. My father needed me with him. But they did not intimate even by so much as a look that they expected me to do anything but go on living in the big city "on them." Result? Of my own accord, not because I thought I *had* to, but with all my heart because I *wanted* to, I went home to stay out the year. I was nineteen, and although I didn't do anything else noticeably unselfish until I became a follower of Jesus Christ at the age of thirty-three, I began to like myself a little once I stopped pushing aside obstacles and people in order to protect myself.

The quality of the love I have always received from Mother and Dad conditioned me for quick, rather natural belief in the love of God. They had made it utterly possible for me to believe that God loved me. I admit to some problems with accepting his discipline, but never his love. My parents were, like yours, not perfect. I'm sure I needed more discipline at their hands. But human love at its very highest will always make mistakes in its actions. It is the *reaction* of love that counts. Actions can be controlled consciously. Reactions show us to be what we truly are.

My parents have loved me freely and in the process conditioned me to love. I am just now, at fifty, beginning to make love my all encompassing aim, but even at the first moment of conscious faith in God, I felt at home. I had grown up in the very atmosphere of giving love. Love that left me free to seek my own fulfillment. Love that did not choke my particular personality.

Love that did not bend me to the image of anyone. Love that never put me in competition with my brother, nor my brother with me.

We all know best the freeing effects of love on our own lives. I have been singularly fortunate to have had an older friend for all the years of my Christian life who also has helped free me by her love. Of all the persons I have met since my conversion, who had known Jesus Christ for many years, the one most important to growth in my new life has been Dr. Anna B. Mow. And looking back over the sixteen years since we met, I can remember going to her only once with a specific problem. The details of the problem have escaped me now and she can't remember that I went to her for help! Ours has not been a counsellor-counsellee relationship in any sense of the word. Her *love* has been the continuing help I needed to go on daring to learn to fly in the love of God on my own. She is unshockable, totally uncondemning, full of the holy humor of God, himself, and she loves me. Of this I have no doubt whatever. Because I know she would never condemn me for anything, I am thrown directly onto God for my need of conviction. Her love stimulates my mind, stretches me inside where I need to be stretched and keeps me actively searching the wider place of freedom in God for more and more knowledge of him. Her love, like the love of my mother, *expects* me into being my best. Sometimes I wish neither of them expected quite so much of me and yet they never *drive* me to keep moving Godward; they *help* me by nurturing my respect for myself, by increasing my utter and profound respect for them both. If those two women think I can do a thing, then God must be involved in it too, and so in quite a surprising childlike way, I simply try it.

Love frees. And freedom incites experiment and experiment opens the door wide to creative living.

A woman wrote, "I have received only one letter from my mother in all the twenty years of my married life in which she did not complain about something."

If I have ever, in all the more than thirty years in which I have lived away from my hometown, received a letter from my mother with a single problem thrown onto my shoulders, I don't remember it. We discuss things in our letters. We are increasingly confidential with each other as the years go by. But complaints? None. This does not mean that my mother is a superior being. It merely means that she loves me in the way that frees: She cares more about my state of mind than she cares about her own.

I have shared the infinite value in my own life from two loves which go on moving toward me, which go on encouraging, stimulating, strengthening me from within. Pages could be filled with illustrations from other lives of the positive and the destructive effects of the right and wrong kind of love. I feel it unnecessary to illustrate further concerning the value to the loved one who *receives* giving love. More has been written on love in our century than at any other time in history. Love is analyzed regularly in the women's magazines, in the Sunday supplements, in book after book. But generally, it is written about from the standpoint of the one who receives the love.

It is important to look at the other side. And what we can see, if we look honestly, and if we *think* as we look, is the even greater freedom which can come to the one who gives love. In the deepest sense, Jesus had to be including the most profound meaning of freedom when he said it is more blessed to give than to receive. *There can be no freer person on earth than the person who has learned how to love.* Why? Because this man or woman is in no danger of suffering from the most binding ailment of all — self pity. If we love, we cannot pity ourselves. It is humanly impossible. If we love, we cannot put ourselves in the position of having to endure hurt feelings, of losing the wasted hours required to nurse and pamper our own touchiness. This kind of freedom is as old as the cross of Christ. It is *older,* because on the cross Christ was demonstrating the love of God as it has always been. Keep this in mind until you reach the last chapter of this book where we will look more closely at the freedom that pours down to us all from the heart that exposed itself to us all when Jesus died. For now, as my friend, Anna Mow says, because of that cross we can all be "God's air-conditioned — living freely in a world of people affected by the weather!"

If a woman truly loves her husband (not just because he is handsome, or rich, or kind, or faithful), she is *free.* And she is free no matter what he does to her because her inner temperature is not disturbed by his actions. She may not like him at all times. She may even want to give him a good shaking now and then, but if she loves him, she will be free to keep her own balance and not increase the confusion and the tension by adding the irritation of her own flailing ego to his. Fighting back does not work, or Jesus was wrong. He told us to love even our enemies, but according to the way most of us act and react, we appear to think him wrong.

"I don't care what Jesus said — he was God and I'm not. I don't intend to sit still for one more session like I had with my mother-in-law last night!"

God never asks us to "sit still." Do you, for one minute think Jesus hung passively on that cross? Do you think he was just hanging there, too weak to defend himself?

Love is always active. It may be utterly silent, but was there ever a silence so full of motion and dynamic activity as the silence Jesus kept before the accusations of Pilate? God does not ask us to be doormats. He asks us to be sons and daughters of the King, but he also expects us to believe that we have all the riches of the King's love on which to draw. Peter drew his sword (he thought) because he loved Jesus and he wanted to strike back at the soldier who arrested Him. Actually, Peter drew his sword because he did not love Jesus with the right kind of love. The big fellow acted in anger, not love, and he ended up making more work for Jesus because Jesus then had to stop in the midst of his own trouble and heal the ear Peter had just cut off.

Whose activity counted? Peter's? Or the Lord's?

Love heals, it never destroys. Peter's act of violence would have led to the bondage of partial deafness; Jesus freed the man to hear again.

Love is not a mere religious doctrine. It is the essence of God himself, because God is love. And God never demands love in return. He never browbeats us into responding from a sense of duty. Real love frees the loved one to respond to the lover.

The wife who refuses to give her husband the freedom his own human dignity demands; the possessive person who feels rejected if he cannot own his friend body, soul, mind and time; the mother who never relinquishes her son or daughter to his or her own life, the minister who forces his flock to agree with his particular Scriptural interpretation or call down his disapproval — all of these bind *themselves* first. And this kind of bondage is choking the life from our society. Each of these touches another life — some touch many other lives. And the choking process goes on, with children, friends, church members, husbands and wives gasping for fresh, free air.

Jesus said:

> If the Son shall make you free, you shall be free indeed. Jn. 8:36

But he was offering to wave no magic wand over our heads so that we could do as we pleased. He also said:

> This is my commandment, That you love one another as I have loved you. Jn 15:12

His love is the love of the cross without self-defense, without self-pity — and totally free.

The freedom *of* love is the freedom *to* love.

*Love does not involve reason
and it knows no boundaries:
not the boundaries of social status,
of economic success or failure,
of likes and dislikes.*

Chapter 5

Love Is Unreasonable

THERE IS CERTAINLY no trick to loving those who interest us, who make us feel important, needed. There is no trick to loving those who give us pleasure, who leave us free. We seek out the people whose prohibitions match ours, just as we seek out those whose lack of prohibition matches ours. If we are comfortable with someone, it is easy to love. It is easy to love a stimulating friend, one who brings out the best in us, the most colorful in us.

But what about the bores? The dullards whose interests seem so narrow we have to work at making conversation? What about the rigid souls who judge us by their own inflexible standards and conditioning? How happy are we in what we call Christian "fellowship" with those whose prohibitions do not match ours? For that matter, how successful are we at loving a tight-lipped, humorless person who not only takes himself too seriously but misses all the sparkle of our great wit? What about the touchy soul around whose personality we must tread softly? The self-righteous one who has yet to admit his first mistake? Are we to love the person who wrongs us? Who cheats us? Who connives to hurt us? Are we to love the neighbor whose life seems motivated by thinking up new ways to torment us? To annoy us at 3 A.M.? Are we to love the neurotic relative who keeps track of our every activity and interprets it according to his or her warped mind? Are we to love the unfaithful friend or husband or wife or child? Are we to love the liar? The gossip? The Communist politician? The Communist soldier whose finger squeezed the trigger that fired the bullet into the body of a loved one?

Yes.

Or Jesus was wrong.

In no way did Jesus describe the *kind* of neighbor we are to love. He did not excuse us from loving the bore, the insensitive, the gossip. He did not locate our neighbors nor confine them to the same street or the same block or even the same country. "God so loved the world," and as far as I can see, Jesus included our world neighbors, friends and enemies, when he said we were to love our neighbors as we love ourselves. In fact, he pinpointed it by telling us to love our enemies outright — those who persecute and mistreat us. Paul was extremely specific to the Romans:

> Owe no one anything, except to love one another: for he who loves his neighbor has fulfilled the law. The commandments, You shall not kill, You shall not steal, You shall not covet, and any other commandment, are summed up in this sentence, You shall love your neighbor as yourself. Love does no wrong to a neighbor; therefore love is the fulfilling of the law.

The Christian who gossips about his neighbor can attend church for the rest of his mortal life, support ten missionaries, keep all his group's prohibitions, read his Bible through twice a year and still not fulfill the law of God. "Love does *no wrong* to a neighbor." No man fulfills the law of God unless he loves his neighbor, or Paul and Jesus were both wrong in their understanding of the law of God.

"We tried to be friends with those new people next door. My husband invited them to go to church with us the very day after they moved in on Saturday. And do you know what the man said to my poor husband? He set down a big box of books he was carrying, looked him right in the eye and said: 'Now, neighbor, if you'd offer me a hand or a cold beer, I'd be tempted to go to church with you some time. Church is the last thing I need right now, man! I'm hot and thirsty and a hand with this box of books or a cold drink sound much better than church, believe me.' Of course, my husband couldn't help him with that box of books — he was dressed for church. But we ignored the beer remark and kept on inviting them to church with us for months — week after week. Do you think they ever went? Even after they got all settled and all and had no more excuses, they didn't go. So, we just do our best to ignore them now. Although it's hard to do when he gets out in the front yard on Sunday and plays touch football with his children!"

The cold beer is not in question here, nor is the Sunday touch football. Love is in question: the limitations of love in the hearts of some church-goers. There are no closed doors in love, no barriers, no limitations.

If there were, God would not — could not love the
world.

A widow, unable to wait for delayed insurance
payments, lost her home because the local banker fore-
closed on her mortgage. Now she baby-sits with the
banker's children and accepts his mingy dollar an hour
with graciousness because she knows love will triumph
in the end — and because she cares, not for her own
pitiable plight, but for the more pitiable state of the
banker's heart. She has learned that God's love never,
never excludes. She has learned and dares to practice
the kind of love that never acts according to the way
it is treated, but acts on what it knows of the heart of
the Father.

The Bible makes it irrevocably clear that we are to
love everyone — friend and enemy, attractive and
despicable, stimulating and boring, rigid and flexible,
loving and unloving, kind and hateful. There are no
exceptions.

> Love does no wrong to a neighbor; therefore love is the
> fulfilling of the law.

These passages from God's Word which instruct us
about the nature of love, which set down so clearly the
characteristics of love, make no exceptions because
they are not directed towards the objects of love. They
are not instructing the loved ones, they are instructing those who do the loving. God's love is never, never
exclusive. It is always totally inclusive and is never
measured nor regulated in any way by the nature of
the loved one. God's love is always and only regulated
by the nature of God himself.

Therefore, our love can only be measured and regu-

lated by our own natures. We can love according to
how much we have permitted God to do for us and in
us. We can love in direct proportion to how much freedom we have accepted at his hand in our own lives.
The religious person who finds it difficult to love those
outside his own persuasion has in part, at least, turned
his back on the One who declared that if He, the Son,
made a man free, he would be free indeed.

Perhaps the great, mainly unconscious flaw in the
nature of the love capacity of the average Christian
is in his mistaken tendency to relate God's love first
of all with what he understands as salvation: his or
her own personal salvation. The person who has,
through mental laziness, superficial teaching, or blindness, come to associate God's love with what God has
done for *him,* cannot come out at the place of total
love because he has gone in at the wrong door. Some
calm, reasoning thought is required here. This in no
way implies that we should diminish God's love by
passing lightly over what he has done for us or by
being ungrateful for our salvation. It does not mean
we should become so academic that we say, in effect:
"Well, God loves the whole world, so of course, he has
done this or that for me. He is a just God and would
make no exceptions." This is true. God makes no exceptions, but tossing our own experience with him into
the general hopper of humanity, robs us of the valid,
energizing personal relationship. Rather, because God
makes no exceptions, we accept as personal — as our
very own — the salvation he offers us, but then we go
on! This is not the place to stop — salvation is not
the place to drive the stakes that mark off God's love.
Salvation is the starting place. We go on from there
to let him change us into something resembling his

own image. To let him recreate us into the image he had in mind for us in the first place. We go on from the initial point of our salvation to learn something of the depth of God's love, so that it can become real in our own lives that he *does love the whole world.* That *he* is in no way exclusive. That his love is a continuing love — a phenomenon that cannot be pinpointed either in time or eternity. A love that goes even beyond the gift of salvation to a human heart.

If we attempt to follow the commandment of Christ to love our neighbors inclusively, with no exceptions, we must neither distort nor upset our progress by the near stupid act of attempting to *like* everyone with no exceptions. It is a constant amazement that so many of us continue to confuse the word *love* with the word *like.* We can no more learn to *like* (be attracted to, find pleasurable) everyone in the world than we can "fly to the moon" without a spaceship. C. S. Lewis wrote:

> . . . our love for ourselves does not mean that we *like* ourselves. It means that we wish our own good. In the same way Christian love for our neighbors is quite a different thing from liking or affection. We 'like' or are 'fond of' some people, and not of others. It is important to understand that this natural 'liking' is neither a sin nor a virtue, any more than your likes and dislikes in food are a sin or a virtue. It is just a fact. But, of course, what we do about it is either sinful or virtuous. . . . Some people are 'cold' by temperament; that may be a misfortune for them, but it is no more a sin than having a bad digestion is a sin; and it does not cut them out from the chance, or excuse them from the duty, of learning charity.

I may not like you and you may not like me, but we *can* love one another. You may not *like* your next door neighbor or your minister's wife or the person who shares your office or your home, but you can *love* them or the God we follow commands the impossible, the unrealistic.

"I don't like anything about my sister-in-law," a young wife said, "but I love my husband, her brother, enough to make an effort to learn to love her. Right now, I can't imagine that I will ever *like* the woman. She's high-brow, a name-dropper, a social climber — everything I dislike. But she grew up with my beloved and because she means something to him, with God's help, I am going to learn to *love* her."

A highly intelligent, well-educated lady told me some time ago that she felt she would never recover from the shock of discovery about herself. For years she had been active in the Human Relations Council, giving her time and her energy and her money to support good relations between the members of the white and Negro races in her southern community. She had made enemies among her white friends by taking part in the Council's work, but she had gone on, believing herself to be acting on the side of love. Then, one day she was at home alone with her Negro maid, when the realization struck her that she did not love her black sister. "I discovered that I 'liked' her — as one 'likes' a breed of dog. I'm mad about French poodles. And when I faced Mary that day in our kitchen, I saw myself as being merely partial to the characteristics of her race! Negroes entertain me — they amuse me. I love to chuckle at their quaint sayings. I admire their courage to sing in the face of hardship, but I enjoy their singing more than I admire their courage. I began to see all my noble efforts in their behalf as mainly rebellion against my stuffy neighbors who still insist that 'Mary is fine in her place.' I did not love Mary. I merely liked her 'breed'."

Liking does not mean loving any more than loving necessarily means liking. When they occur together, it is a beautiful thing; meaningful relationships result — genuine attachments that matter for all the years of our lives, even when distance separates us. But they do not occur simultaneously every time. It is, rather, the exception when we both like and love another person.

Now, Jesus said nothing about learning to like someone. He was too realistic for that. On occasion, when we get to know a person whom we disliked on sight, we learn to like him or her. But there is no instruction in the Bible concerning our likes and dislikes because, as Dr. Lewis said, to like someone is no more a virtue than to like a certain food. We should, of course, cultivate our creative likings both for certain foods and for certain people, *but we are to love everyone,* right or wrong.

Liking denotes willing preference on our part. Loving involves us, even against our wills. I cannot believe that Jesus *liked* the smug members of the Sanhedrin who stood jeering beneath his cross. I know that he loved them. He was hanging there proving his love, demonstrating the very heart of God to them as well as to his mother and to his beloved disciple, John.

Jesus must have *liked* John, but he did not love him any more than he loved Judas.

In *The Gospel According to Peanuts,* Robert L. Short wrote:

There are several reasons why "what we preach"

turns out to be comic or "folly" or "the foolishness of God," to use Paul's terms. The first involves the very nature of love . . . itself. In the history of western literature there is probably a no more popular subject for comedy than the complete blindness of love, of the lover who insists on making a fool of himself simply because his passions have the upper hand over his reason. Both love and faith can never give a *reason* for their love; they can only say, "This is my beloved."

Love has no reason beyond its own nature. Where would even the most lovable among us be if God required a reason for loving us?

Love does not involve reason and it knows no boundaries: not the boundaries of social status, of economic success or failure, of likes or dislikes. And it is never, never exclusive. Love cannot be trapped or cornered behind a barrier of race, or political affiliation or religious emphasis.

Love is always free to love and its arms are always stretched as wide as the cross toward anyone who needs to be loved — and that includes everyone born into our world.

*The love we give can only be creative
if it is based on God's
idea of love, not ours.*

Chapter 6

Do We Love Only the Idea of Love?

ALMOST EVERYONE CAN BE said to consider himself an authority on love. That is, if we regard not only the deluge of books and articles on the ancient subject, but the haphazardly overheard comments of our friends and neighbors and the other customers at super markets and laundermats — and especially at the beauty parlors.

"I'd say, if you ask me, that he never did love her. No man could love a woman and embarrass her in public the way he does."

"Oh, she loves him all right — in direct proportion to the bulge in his wallet."

"Of course I love my children, but the way they look with their hair down in their eyes and wearing those strange clothes, I sometimes have trouble showing it. My son adored his cowboy boots when he was six, but he seems to adore them more now that he's sixteen. I know if I really love my teen-agers, I'll overlook this phase. But I'm in a phase too — wondering just how far love is supposed to stretch!"

"I know my friend loves me. She's so good when I'm sick and all. But do you think we laugh at the people we love? When I get anxious or worried about something, Helen invariably laughs at me! As though she knew some special spiritual secret I didn't know. Do you call that love?"

In the first chapter of his book, *The Ability To Love*, Dr. Allan Fromme poses the question *what is love?* and then writes:

> In a sense, anyone can answer this question; everyone today is an expert on love. Each of us feels in his heart that he is a good lover — or that he could be if only he had the right person to love or the right atmosphere for love. It is very much like what we feel about our ability to drive an automobile. No one says, 'I'm a less-than-average driver.'
>
> And so it is with love. No one admits even to himself that he is a less-than-average lover, or merely an average lover. Each of us thinks of himself as tender, sensitive, full of insight and understanding, capable of great passion and complete devotion. We may admit certain reservations about our capacity for love, but usually because of defects in the object of our love or in the circumstances, and never or almost never in ourselves.

Why is this? Why do we seemingly contradict ourselves where love is concerned? Why do we feel we are love specialists and still give way to inner doubts about the reality of the loves we experience, both in ourselves and in our loved ones? Do I really love her enough? Does he really love me? Is the love I feel for my teen-ager so shallow I permit the way he wears his hair and his high-heeled boots to shake it? Oh, I know it's only a phase . . . like the phases husbands go through when a big deal is on . . . like the phases wives go through when a charity drive is on. We know and we don't know about love.

Why this seeming paradox concerning an emotion as old as human history itself?

Obviously our varying degrees of human selfishness are relevant here. We understand a subject as we master it. Few of us have mastered love. We analyze it as a psychic phenomenon, we urge it as a religious doctrine. We learn its principles, but when it comes to the application of these principles, we are far more authoritative on the way other people love than on our own ability to love.

This is one reason for the seeming paradox where love is concerned. But there is more.

It seems to me that we need to explore our own concept of love. Is it love that holds us? Is it love that motivates our reactions, our actions? Or is it merely the idea of love?

Our idea of love?

Dr. Fromme says that it

> is far easier to tell stories about love, to savor love in one or another artistic form, to muse and dream about love than actually to answer the searching questions we all raise about love. What is love? Why do we fall in love? Why is love so often associated with anguish, disappointment, and disillusionment? Is love different for men and women? What can we do to maintain love, to make it grow? And where does the power of love come from, that it arouses such deep feelings in us?

In no period of history has love been spoken of or written about as in ours. No period, it seems, (if we look around us) has asked less of love than ours. We have given the *name* of love to a vague, contagious obsession which springs in our time from the romantic novel and spreads through our films and TV fictions until we no longer recognize the obsession as vague — merely contagious. Our idea of love is worn so thin that we warp the lives of our children and break up homes and friendships and business partnerships because other people "are not acting according to what we are certain love is." That we have permitted ourselves to be satiated by a delusion never enters our minds.

"A woman expects certain things of the man who claims to love her! Of course my husband is a good provider, and I know he has never been unfaithful to me. But how does a woman know she's loved if he never remembers a birthday, never takes her out to dinner, never tells her she's beautiful?"

"Love? My parents kicked the whole love bit a long time ago. They're ancient — both in their forties. How could they know anything about love?"

"The fact that my colored cook wouldn't think of coming to my front door has nothing whatever to do with the fact that I love her! These Civil Rights agitators don't know anything about real love. What right have they to say that my idea of love is any less than theirs?"

Do we love our idea of love?

Isn't it about time we began to discover love as it really is? Love as God himself demonstrated it to be as he hung on the Cross? If the introduction of God into the discussion of love disturbs you, dulls your interest, you can be absolutely sure that you have not examined love as it really is.

We have so sentimentalized our concept of love that it bears almost no resemblance to the original. We have taken the word of the authors of romantic novels and motion pictures and TV and perfume ads above the word of God himself on the subject. The Bible declares that God *is* love. How closely does your concept of love resemble the love of God? We tend almost entirely to judge the quality of love according to the way it makes the loved one *feel*. A woman knows she is loved *if* she is made to feel beautiful, remembered, needed. And all of these things are certainly a part of the experience of being loved. But to judge love by *feeling* is our big error and the point at which we turn aside from God's original concept.

I wrote in my book, *The Wider Place,* about the fact that my father didn't remember his wedding anniversary once in forty-three years without a reminder. I can think of no better illustration here. His forgetfulness did not cause Mother to feel unloved. She didn't marry him so that he would remember the date. She married him because she loved him. His forgetfulness had nothing whatever to do with his love, or hers. It had only to do with a personality defect in the man, and who among us has none?

The theme of *The Wider Place* is freedom. There is no better way to point out the freedom of love than to use this simple illustration again. Our idea of love, based on over-sentimentality and romance, *binds*. Real love *frees* both parties to love more and still more and still more. As long as we are expecting, even demanding, that someone conform to our idea of love, we clamp chains on the loved one's heart. When we begin, however slowly, to free the loved one by acting ourselves on love as it is shown to us in the heart of God, we set the loved one free to begin to love us more.

Love is not necessarily rational. Real love does have directly to do with the "foolishness of God." Real love loves for love's sake and not because the loved one is lovable. Real love begins steadily to remake the loved one, to recreate the beloved into being more loveable — easier to love. Re-creation and redemption go hand in hand here. "We love God because he first loved us." God had first to love us into being able to love him in return. This is the continuing, redemptive principle underlying the authentic love of God. But as long as we are living our daily lives by the principle of *our idea of love*, it cannot work anything but hardship and confusion and misunderstanding.

It is easy to spot those few among our friends and relatives who really love us. There are half a dozen persons on whom I can depend to love me regardless of my attention to them. They think first of how busy I might be, not of how much they would like to hear from me. There are others on whom I can depend to be offended and impatient if I don't answer a letter when they expect me to answer it. Over and over I receive mail which says in effect: "Don't wait so long to answer the next time. We thought you loved us. Remember now, we love you."

This is their *idea* of love. I appreciate their interest in me, but I am chained by it when my desk is piled with unanswered mail, when I've a book or two in the works and they still expect me to drop it all and focus my attention on them because they "love me."

"I honestly think I would have made the honor roll this year if I'd been able to stay at school for the Thanksgiving holiday to study. But Mother insisted that I must come home and stuff myself with turkey. I gained 3 pounds and missed the honor roll. Mother said she missed me so much she would get sick if I didn't come. I didn't want guilt to carry around along with my heavy curriculum next semester, so I went and lost out."

Ignorantly, innocently, perhaps, this mother "loved" from her idea of love and the student daughter paid for it.

Only God's idea of love frees the loved one to be and to do his best. Only God's idea of love is creative. Only God's idea of love stimulates the response our hearts were fashioned to give. If this love-deluded mother had caught on to the principle of God-love with her daughter, she would have found her daughter arranging things so she could come home the next time without coercion. We were created in the first place to respond to love. We all need to be loved and we all long for it. But we all kick against the goads of being possessed, of being "loved" according to someone's idea of love. It is only in the realm of God-love that we feel at home. It is only in the realm of God-love that we can be free. God-love does not generate false guilt. Real love, God-love, relieves the human heart of guilt; it never creates false guilt by demanding for itself.

The love we give can only be creative if it is based on God's idea of love, not ours.

*Learning to love with God's love
requires no special feeling on our part.
It requires only doing . . .
We begin to learn to love
by practicing.*

Chapter 7

How Do We Learn to Love?

BEFORE WE CAN truly make love our aim, we must first discover where we have been living by *unlove*.

We are all guilty of *unlove* even toward those we love best. To deny this is to begin at the point of unreality. Every parent and every child and every friend and every husband and wife acts in *unlove* some of the time. The record must be straight here. *Everyone* needs to learn to love more creatively, more consistently.

But can we learn this? Is love a skill which can be acquired by practice?

No and Yes.

Notice that the No precedes the Yes. There is a definite reason for this. At this place in my own life, I do not see how love itself can be *learned*, as one learns the multiplication tables or the structure of the atom. The years ahead may show this to be an oversimplification, but I am more convinced now than I was eighteen years ago, when I saw it first, that love is always a gift. Real love is always a gift from God: a gift of himself. Paul, who was apparently not a loving person by nature, reminds us that "the love of God is shed abroad in our hearts by the Holy Spirit." Real love is always giving love, and the gift is the very love of the Giver, himself.

When God comes, in the person of his Holy Spirit, to live his life *in* the actual life of the believer, he brings his love along. If he did not, he would not bring himself: God is love. God cannot come without love because he is love. He is not only love, he, the Holy Spirit, is the teacher of love. Jesus said the Holy Spirit would lead us into all truth. So, according to my present sight of it, real love is first of all a gift from God of himself and our practice of love — our learning how to love — is the result of his teaching us how to make use of his gift.

Now, this seems to imply that only the "advanced" Christian can learn how to love. Perhaps it is true that only those closely related to Christ in their daily lives know how to love steadily, day in and day out, finding it increasingly easy to concentrate upon the loved ones rather than upon themselves. There is no power loose in our universe strong enough to overrule our self-concern but love for God. Therefore, if a missionary in the Congo is responding to God first, he or she will find it possible to go on demonstrating love in the midst of the kind of horror in the civil uprising that took the life of Dr. Paul Carlson and so many of God's other friends in and near Stanleyville. These men and women loved God more than they loved themselves. And so they died in a kind of perplexing triumph — weary, anxious, frightened, but in an attitude of love.

They were not motivated by the exhilaration of knowing themselves to be potential martyrs for the cause of Christ. There was no time nor energy for false stimulation as they passed one terror-filled day after another under the almost constant harrassment of the half-crazed Simbas. They were able to continue planning such meals as they could manage, bathing when possible, caring for their children and even sleeping periodically, because they loved God. And they loved God, not because they were "spiritual specialists" but because they had begun to learn (under the direct guidance of the Spirit of God) something of the quality of his love for them and for their enemies.

Everyone will always be learning to love. It will never be an accomplished fact on this earth because there are more dimensions in the love of God than the human heart can contain or comprehend. But because life in Christ is eternal, continuing, not limited by time or circumstance, and because God's concern that we be taught is unending, the learning process goes on, interrupted only by our times of unwillingness.

It would not be at all surprising to find the learning process going on after life on this earth. Most of us, I'm sure, hope this is true. With God, even completion is incomplete, in that there is no end to his greatness, to his mind, to his love. He is the beginning and the end, and this gives an expectation for the future of life with him that far surpasses streets of gold and gates of pearl. When the heart and the mind stop learning, life stops. And with God, life is eternal — both in quality and length. There is no joy comparable to the joy of discovering something new from God, about God. If the continuing life is a life of joy, we will go on discovering, learning.

So, those who are steadily learning how to love are enabled to do this because the very love of God, himself, has been *put into* our hearts. We do not have to whip up feelings of affection or emotion which we might recognize as love. Love is already there if Christ is there.

But what of those who seem to love more consistently, with more selfless devotion to their fellow man than some Christians we know? Are these people freaks? Is the quality of their love not valid? Are they silent believers? Frequently, yes. And perhaps even more frequently, those who are not considered Christian by other Christians merely express their faith in terms so different they are passed by unrecognized. Still, I believe there is one more possible explanation as to why certain men and women seem able to love even though they make no verbal confession of faith in Jesus Christ. The possible explanation is simply this: God is far more powerful and his love far more penetrating than any of us can believe! We know that no man comes to the Father except through Jesus Christ, but as C. S. Lewis has pointed out, we have no way of knowing how many Christ has somehow reached without our knowing or even recognizing it. If there is but one God and if Jesus Christ is his Son and if the fruits of the Spirit of the one God show up in a man's life, the man who loves must have had some kind of touch from the Eternal. When Paul preached at Mars Hill, he hinted strongly at this freeing truth:

> Men of Athens, I perceive that in every way you are
> very religious. For as I passed along, and observed the
> objects of your worship, I found also an altar with this
> inscription, 'To an unknown god.' What therefore you
> worship as unknown, this I proclaim to you.

Paul did not tell them glibly that they worshipped false gods. He had seen too clearly the person of the one God, had too decisively experienced the power of this one God even to admit the existence of false gods! Paul simply said that he would tell them the name of the God whom they called *unknown*. When a human heart is turned, however slightly and however erroneously toward the Eternal One, He is found to be already in movement toward that human heart. We dare not limit the living, all loving, totally involved God.

Whatever of love has touched a man's life, that life has been touched by God. His theology may be distorted or even nonexistent, but God has never been and will never be limited or hampered by man's attempt to explain him. He will move heaven and earth to make himself clear in Jesus Christ, so that our faith can take root in the absolute and grow, but he could not draw back from any of his created children because he did not find them theologically astute. So that, whatever of God has touched a man's life, that life has been touched by love. By the same token, whatever of love involves a man, that man has consciously or unconsciously been touched by God. John said it with all clarity, seemingly unafraid that the "saints" would disapprove:

> Beloved, let us love one another; for love is of God, and
> he who loves is born of God and knows God. He who
> does not love does not know God; for God is love.

Anyone who can show genuine love has some conscious or unconscious contact with God, so it is healthy for the Christian to look around at the quality of love he sees among those who do not adhere to the letter of his Christian persuasion. The Christian should be able to love more freely because he has direct access to the very love that stretched itself on Calvary. He does not need to develop a love of his own that somehow resembles Calvary love. He has it there already available.

So, while love is a gift from God himself, we can learn increasingly to participate in it, and in the participating discover more about its Source. We can learn how to give and not to clutch for ourselves. How to bless and not curse. We can learn how to love our enemies and do good toward those who spitefully use us. And we have at hand the only kind of love which can weather such involvement: the love that says, "Father, forgive them . . ."

How do we go about learning to make use of God's love in the daily round?

By beginning. And the only way to begin is to open ourselves to more knowledge of the true nature of this love. It must be remembered that God's love is not just a higher quality than human love. It is different. In no way does it rule out human love or denegate it. God's love, when it is permitted to complete itself in a human heart, is always mingling itself with our human love. God is not proud. He will love quickly and gladly through the sometimes shoddy, inadequate human efforts we grant him. Love is his nature. God cannot deny himself and so he is always more than willing. His *will* is not involved. Not as we think of an act — a separate act of will on Monday or Thursday. God never has to stop and think about whether he will love or not. He cannot stop loving because he *is* love. If he stopped loving he would stop being. His love cannot die anymore than he can die.

We must learn about God's heart as it really is in Jesus Christ and only then can we begin to love as Christ commands us to love. We flinch and turn the page when we read that our Lord instructed us to love those who kick us around. We cannot. And Jesus did not fling out these hard words with no preparation at hand for us. Remember, he said: "Learn of me." There is no other way.

Some of us are more naturally inclined to be loving, but this has nothing whatever to do with virtue. No human love stands up every minute through every crisis without striking back. Only God's love does this, and we cannot expect ourselves·to know the fine points of loving with a love about which we are ignorant. We must go on learning of Jesus Christ, and, as we do, inevitably we will be learning the nature of the love of God. One day we will realize that we are beginning to learn *how to love* with God's love.

Learning to love with God's love requires no special feeling on our part. It requires only doing. No one always feels like showing selfless love, and it is here we stumble most often. We want to *feel* loving. We want to anticipate at least social martyrdom if we reach toward some unlovely person to bless and not to curse. We prefer some feeling of exhilaration for our sacrifice. And demanding a particular *feeling* is one sure way to halt the learning process.

"Too many years have gone by. My wife has thrown too many tantrums. My love has been dead too long. I can't love her any more and yet I have to consider the children. I'd settle now for just being able to stand the sight of her. But how?"

By doing. By acting. We will never believe until we try it out — God's love changes not only us but the other person. By small, hard-to-come-by acts of love, this man began to be able to "stand the sight" of his wife. He gritted his teeth and *acted,* and slowly, slowly he had to admit that she wasn't quite as obnoxious as he had thought her to be. What we recognize as "romance" did not return. It seldom does. But love took over — God's love, through a man who made an honest effort to act on what he came to believe about the quality of that love. After a while, there was even some feeling in his efforts: "The first time I noticed that I was changing toward her too came when I found myself wondering if she would really like the pot of tulips I picked up on my way home from work one night. Up to then, I had simply begun holding her chair at the table again when she sat down, bringing her a small gift now and then or helping with the dishes — all definite acts of my will. Sometimes I felt as though I were testing God and I suppose I was in a way. But then the recognizable feeling of near-affection came, and I saw that I was changing too."

We can begin to learn to love by practicing. There it is in black and white. Once we have caught on to something of the nature of God's love operative in us, we can begin to use it creatively only by practice. God designed our minds to function best through regular exercise of our wills. This characteristic of our humanity is in itself, neutral. If we practice love, we become loving. If we practice hate, we become hateful. We choose the nature of our exercise. Only the overly-sentimental person goes about with his head in a bag believing that all people are loving at heart, that all people are good. We are not. All people are selfish at heart. Christian love is never sentimentalized love, it is always realistic. But far from ruling out honest sentiment, it keeps it strong and lasting. There is nothing cold about the love of God, although some would consider a love that had to be exercised as disagreeable, almost pedantic. This kind of observation is, of course, the direct and immediate consequence of over-sentimentality.

We can, any of us, begin to learn the quality of the love of God. It has already been demonstrated beyond question, beyond confusion in the life and death of Jesus Christ. And once we see something of its quality, then we can begin to act on what we have learned.

If God's love has done a great thing for us, we should have no hestitancy about sharing it. Perhaps we dare to learn how to love in direct proportion to how much we dare to admit what his love has done for us. In direct proportion to our own need fulfilled. Those who have never gone to God with smashed hearts, in desperate life and death need of his love, quite naturally don't bother to give love to others.

"We love God because he first loved us." He loves us into loving him. We can go on practicing love in our own small spheres until we have loved ourselves into loving.

Part III

"For God so loved the world that
he gave his only Son, that whoever
believes in him should not perish
but have eternal life." (RSV)

Only God could know what new things
might come to our world
if men and women dared to learn
to love enough to stand for
a little while in another's shoes.

Chapter 8

Loving Enough to Identify

W E LEARN TO BELIEVE by believing. We
learn to love by loving. The practice of acting
on a certain thing, even (or especially) when feeling
is absent, embodies the entire "how" of growth. That
growth is irrevocably involved with love, Paul knew.
His magnificently written letter to the Corinthians
sets down the characteristics of love and flows directly
into a profound description of true maturity:

> When (love) the perfect comes, the imperfect will pass
> away. When I was a child, I spoke like a child, I thought
> like a child, I reasoned like a child; when I became a
> man, I give up childish ways.

Learning to love is maturity. One cannot come without the other. Perhaps it would be more accurate to
say that maturity is the prime characteristic of love.
Maturity concerns itself for the other person and
ceases to grab, as a child grabs, for its own way, its
own pleasure.

Surely, maturity was shown at its supreme moment in human history at Calvary. Christ's kind of maturity is not possible for man on this earth, but the goal is ours. More than a goal — the potential for maturity is in us all, particularly if Christ is given the freedom to be himself in us.

And only the maturing human being can learn to identify. Only the maturing human being will bother, will even want to take the time or the effort required to stand where someone else is standing.

"I wish they'd stop printing those horrible war pictures on the front pages of our newspapers and in our magazines! It just turns my stomach. There's nothing I can do about it, so I've just tried to stop looking at them. Every day another picture of some poor American boy over there in that foreign land suffering and dying in the heat and stink among strangers! And for what? It's all I can do to keep from thinking all night long that it could be my nephew — he's the right age."

Certainly no one urges morbid dwelling on the ugly realities of any human tragedy, but creative identification is in no way morbid. Of course, there is nothing this woman can do about the suffering among those whose age and the accident of sex has forced upon them, but this does not preclude identification. I know of no better prod to active, creative prayer than to open a newspaper to a photograph of human suffering. Single-handed, none of us can stop a war, but single-handed one praying heart can move the hand of God. One moment's identification with the American soldier who writes of his own personal dedication to freedom for all men of this earth can cause us to remember our freedom. The kind of freedom unknown to over half of the people of our earth. To remember to cherish the freedom we take for granted, to remember to give thanks for it as we ask God's intervention in every effort to block the spread of human liberty. Prayer is not merely a part of ritual. Prayer is contact with the living God, and one prayer prayed in identification with another human being in his pain and discomfort can loose the power of the very God of love into our loveless world. We have all confidence in radio waves and electronic communications from the moon, but we feel feeble and helpless and rebel when "all we can do is pray." It is quite possible that prayer involves (contains) all the power known scientifically to man, along with all he will ever discover. Who knows for certain? But then how many of us have really tried the power of prayer born in the often difficult but always fertile ground of true identification?

Every moment of his life on earth, Jesus identified both with God and with man. He *was* both God and man. And he remained true to his whole nature. He set the pattern for us here: It is possible (fantastic as it seems) for us to become in a definite sense, something of God as well as man. In no way does this rob Jesus of his Deity or the singularity of his divine nature. He was perfect Man and God. This we can never be in our human state. But the only sense I've ever been able to make from his being called "the second Adam" is that in Jesus of Nazareth, God is reminding his lost and sinning loved ones of what they threw away in Eden. Reminding us that we, too, because of Jesus Christ, can be whole again: our human natures with the divine nature restored to us through faith in him.

Jesus could have done nothing that he did if active identification had not been at the heart of his every movement on earth — at the center of his every thought. He kept his identity with the Father intact. They were one. There was a question from the cross: "My God, my God, why hast thou forsaken me?" But it was the question of a loving Son to his Father. A question that must have sprung from the pain and stress on his humanity of the horror-filled moment. There *was* this one question, but there was never a break in the love-relationship — the identification between Father and Son.

We are here concerned more directly, though, with the constancy, the faithfulness of Jesus' identification with us. God had guided the Israelites by pillars of cloud and fire and burning bushes and waters that opened before them. He had ordained prophets to tell them to live at peace with the Lord God. It is no wonder at all that motion picture spectaculars are produced from the dramatic, mystifying, sometimes shocking stories of the Old Testament. The people were primitives and God was acting with them as he knew them to be. But in his time, he began the slow, steady unfolding of redemption. And when God knew (for reasons we still don't grasp) the time was right, the great, quiet, unobtrusive, almost secret miracle took place. He came himself to live among us on our planet in the person of a Baby called Jesus, who was born in a stable of good, but ordinary Jewish parents. Born in the night with no fanfare except the singing of angels, heard apparently only by those who had managed to keep some contact with the God of Abraham and Isaac and Jacob.

The dramatic efforts to bring man back into the fellowship of obedience stopped, and God, instead of signs in the skies, began the humanly understandable act of identification. When Jesus came, God came. The God of all the wide-flung universe came to live simply among his creatures, as one of them. He kept his Deity intact. To me, this is not merely a theological doctrine of Christianity, it could have been no other way. No man could have lived as Jesus lived — all perfection, all gentleness, all humility, all love — if he had not remained God *even as he became man.* He remained God, but he entered that first Christmas night into the supreme act of identification.

Jesus identified with us in our temptations as he endured his own in the wilderness. On the cross, he hung in the gap between man's suffering and the knowledge of God's love. He is now free to expect us to accept his comfort, to thrust our faith into the reality of his understanding. Because of the suffering — both physical and mental — of Jesus Christ (God himself) no one ever needs to believe himself cut off from God by pain of any kind. We may question God's presence, because we cannot always sense it when our feelings are saturated with pain, but we need not doubt it. Here, Jesus may have made his supreme identification with us. In response to our questioning the presence of God in our human pain, he may have knocked over the last barrier to faith: the last credible barrier. Because we are not asked to follow an unfeeling Savior, a Savior immune to pain. We are not even asked to follow an *unquestioning* Savior. Jesus did cry out "Why?" from the depths of his own pain. And in some way, those of us who have been forced by our own need to permit him to give extra of his love know that because he cried out, we need never do it again. Jesus has so completely identified with the human predicament that he has even cried "Why?" for us.*

Jesus Christ knows what it is like to feel pain and he also knows what it is like to feel alone on the earth — and tempted. He has entered into the pressure-filled world of temptation with us and so we can know he does not condemn us for being tempted. To prove it, he was tempted also. Because he did not give in to his own temptations, he can identify with us when we too make use of the power of God to resist. He has identified with us in all things. Jesus understands the squeeze on the human spirit from poverty. From what society calls "a poor background." He was born in a stable into a simple provincial family, and he grew up in a hill-country community where some of the gossips went right on believing him to be illegitimate. Throughout his earthly life he had no home of his own, no place to lay his head other than a hillside or the bank of a stream or a borrowed bed. Even in death, he was laid in a borrowed tomb.

On the cross, in a way we can only wonder at, Jesus identified also with the sin of man. "He became sin" . . . this pure Son of God. It is quite possible that he did not bleed to death nor die from the physical brutality of the cross itself. The weight of the sin of the human race, coupled with the resultant burden of its guilt, could have killed him. Could literally have caused his human heart to burst under the strain. But even as he died in his physical body, *he was identifying.* No human being escapes death. I will die and you will

---

* See *What Is God Like?* Eugenia Price, (Zondervan)

die. Jesus died too, so we would know that he knows what death is like.

But the identification did not stop there. It is as though it only began. On the morning of Jesus' resurrection, he identified with the joy of the few disciples — the women, who found his tomb empty. He anticipated their joy in fact, even as he shared it. His first words to them: "Oh, joy!" shouted to every human heart that has ever experienced joy, that God has known it too. God himself, in Jesus Christ, shouted for joy when he rose from the dead in the light-filled, tangled garden where the empty tomb stood useless forevermore.

When we recover from an illness, the sheer joy of our returning health is almost more than we can bear. God knows how we feel then too. He walked out into the sunlit garden alive and well again and he shouted for joy.

And the great identification goes on, more amazingly now, an even more astounding proof of his love. Because day by day throughout every age of human history, the same Spirit that rose in Jesus Christ that first Easter morning, will live in daily identification with every human being who walks our earth. God is every minute totally aware of each one of us. Totally aware in intense concentration and love. It is true that when we receive him, when we link our lives and our eternal destinies with his, only then is the identification complete. *He waits for us to decide this.* But when we do, the delicate minute by minute involvement — the perfect identification begins and it never ends. No man passes through any area of his life, happy or tragic, without the attention of God with him.

Even if a man hates God, God's identification goes on. He hung on his cross for the smug Pharisees, who maneuvered his death, and for the Roman soldiers, who drove the nails, with the same love flowing from his heart toward them as flowed toward his mother and his beloved disciple, John, who stood grieving as he died. *God does not love Christians best, he simply has more access to them.* His opportunities to show us the creative, redemptive quality of his love are merely greater, more frequent, if we have made him welcome in our lives.

But God's willingness, even eagerness to identify is not diminished by lack of faith. Nothing changes him. And fortunately for all of us, he never portions his love out according to our behavior. Not according to our loyalty to any church, not according to our faithfulness, not according to our service or our tithes and offerings or our spiritual growth. God loves because he is love, and for no other reason.

This sets us free as nothing else could. And if we would use the minds he gave us, we would have to use no will power at all to stop judging each other. We would stop expecting God to make pets of those who serve him. He did not love Dr. Paul Carlson any more than he loved the Simba whose bullets cut him down as he was attempting to climb a wall to safety. Why did Charles Davis make it over that wall and Dr. Paul Carlson did not? Did God play favorites? We should give thanks for safety, and we should give thanks for lack of it, or the apostle Paul was wrong when he instructed us to give thanks in and for everything.

Who can explain one death and another life spared?

No one should try. We play God when we do, or we somehow (perhaps innocently) claim special dispensation when we imply that God had a reason for an accidental death or a life accidentlly spared. If we do not believe God works in the accidental, in the haphazard, then we diminish his power, his interest in his loved ones.

From God's side, for the believer, there are no accidents, but for us to attempt to encompass this intellectually is sheer madness. It has been known to drive men mad to try.

We cannot understand many of the Whys that rise in our hearts, but we can be sure that God is every minute, still identifying — not only with our Whys, but with our feeling that he has forsaken us when our questions are not answered. Jesus asked Why? of the Father; but this did not stop him from quietly committing his spirit into the Father's hands.

His identification with us when at last we grow quiet is as complete as with our cry of doubt. We miss much when we fail to remember that he is identifying with our joy as well as our sorrow, and this is unfair to the God who created us with a capacity for joy.

God alone can love enough for the complete identification of Jesus Christ. Only he can identify with us all in all things. But his love *has been shed* abroad in our hearts, and so we can *learn* to identify as we permit ourselves to be taught by Love himself.

What might happen in our troubled world if only a few thousand men and women learned how to love enough to begin to identify with the rest of the people of the world? What might happen if only a few were willing to learn to love enough to stand, however briefly, in the place of those who suffer for any reason? To stand in the place of the hungry, the rioting, the lonely, the frightened, the bigoted, the homeless whom God loves as much as he loves us.

Only God could know what new things might come to our world if men and women dared to learn to love enough to stand for a little while in one another's shoes. To identify, as Christ did, when he came to live in our world with us as a Man.

God alone is trustworthy,
and we show our love for him
in direct proportion to the extent
of our trust in him.

Chapter 9

Loving Enough to Trust

IT APPEARS THAT WE all have a tendency to
slip to one side of the true meaning of the word
trust. Especially when we speak or think of trusting
God. The slip to one side occurs when we "trust" him
as a last resort. Trust, in reality an active word —
filled with personal involvement on our part — then
becomes a way of avoiding action, a means of *not* becoming involved. The easy way out.

It seems well to have this straight at the outset of
any consideration of the relationship between loving
and trusting. There are times when it is best for us
to *do nothing* in a situation requiring trust in God. But
doing nothing does not necessarily imply inactivity.
There is an activity of the spirit, silent, unseen, which
must be the dynamic of any form of truly creative,
fruitful trust. When we commit a predicament, a possibility, a person to God in genuine confidence, we do
not merely step aside and tap our foot until God comes
through. We remain involved. We remain in contact

with God in gratitude and praise. But we do this without anxiety, without worry.

Does this involve love? Entirely. True, authentic trust in God implies love. Not the mere giving of affection, as we so often think of love, but both sides of the coin: the freedom love gives and the love that always results from freedom.

God's love embodies both.

Our human love can learn to embody both.

For example, I fail to see how anyone can trust a God he doesn't know and love. The new Christian *feels* as though he knows God. In a very definite sense, he does. The light has only recently fallen upon him; the glow is still everywhere. The contrast is as clear as day and night. There is a singular, uncomplicated *knowing* that possesses a new believer and it is, at first, easy for him to trust God. There is a singular, uncomplicated, child-like love invading his entire self — and *love trusts*. There is the first overwhelming sense of freedom from old patterns and old guilts — the wings are still on the feet from having flown over the last mile home. In the heart of the new Christian is the very atmosphere of trust, of confidence.

All of these — freedom, love, knowing — breed trust. And the ease with which a new believer trusts is normal, entirely plausible.

The years go by and he is no longer a new believer. The newness wears off. He has been exposed to other, staler Christians. He has gotten his mind and attention on his work, his human responsibilities, his daily round. God has not changed. God is just as trustworthy as ever, and in a sense, neither has the believer changed. But the first clarity with which he saw the utter trustworthiness of God, the first continuing confidence in the love of God, the first burst of inner-freedom diminishes. He remembers how to worry again, how to be anxious. He is reminded often because the old patterns turn up, still unbroken; the old prejudices recur, the old tendencies to conform. They are not as strong as before, and there is a new power available to defeat them — to wipe them out, but their tracks are still there, and where he once worried and grew anxious, he does so again.

What of the believer's "new life?" Weren't all things made new when he believed? Yes. But God made our minds with the ability to retain. Our behavior patterns actually make tracks in our minds, and a new spirit within us does not wipe out these tracks. This is not the purpose of the life of Christ within us. His purpose is to act *with* us in our circumstances, guiding and empowering us into the making of new tracks — new, straight paths. He does not merely wipe out, he replaces. And many of us get caught here — *not thinking*. We fall into unnecessary times of doubt, into unnecessary days and nights of anxiety and worry. We long for the first days of our faith, when trusting seemed so easy. We mistakenly believe ourselves to be guilty of having slipped away from God. And if we think this way long enough, we can slip away!

Is there a solution to this problem? Is there a way to avoid tumbling into this common pit of misunderstanding? I believe there is. We can all begin, at whatever state in which we find ourselves, to make an honest attempt at discovering the relationship between love and trust.

We tend to push aside, with what we call "humility," any concentration on our love for God. Of course, our love for him is an imperfect, half-formed, immature love. If it weren't, there would be no selfishness abroad on the earth. The truly intelligent person knows he does not love God enough — does not yet know how, and sometimes does not even care to respond to God. Our worship is routine and often shallow; familiar words mouthed in creeds and hymns of a Sunday morning. Our prayer-life is a half-life, generally on the surface, asking favors for ourselves and our loved ones. Our obedience is spasmodic — suspended when it costs too much or seems expedient. Even those who serve God tend to "serve better" and with more willing hearts if they are the speakers of the hour or the chairmen of the committees. We all fall short of adequate love for the God who loves us with a total, pure, entirely commited love.

And yet, we do love him. In varying degrees, to be sure. But God has his people across the world, and they are men and women and children and young people who truly love him. Who truly love His Person, not just a religious concept of deity. The love may be unduly narrow, as a result of religious conditioning — it may feel it is responding to God by living an unnecessarily restricted life, but God's people *do love him*, do sometimes die for their love of him, do act toward him with what they know of love. And God looks on the human heart, not on the printed "statement of faith" at the top of the masthead of whatever religious magazine his loved ones happen to read. Every Christian, who shows love and compassion and mercy and understanding toward another human being, shows his love for God. Every Christian, who chooses to keep rancor and venom out of a conversation about politics or the Civil Rights issue or the various translations of the Bible, is showing his love for God. "Blessed are the peacemakers," Jesus said. He did not say "blessed are those who fight and argue for what they believe to be right."

We do love God and instead of sidestepping mention of our love for him, we should concentrate on it, cultivate it. However small and pinched our love is, it can grow. However deep and wide and sacrificial it is, it can grow. Where there is life there is the potential for growth and where God is, *life is*.

In a later chapter, we will examine the need for self-love — true self-love. And surely part of a God-like regard for ourselves is a balanced, feasible regard for our love for him. Instead of "pious" dwelling on the inadequacy of our love, we need to begin to declare it in our actions. Of course it isn't enough, my love for God. Of course it isn't enough, your love for God. But we do love him, and we need to let it be known.

The most effective, distinctly Christian way to show our love for God is to trust him.

If the world sees us worrying, biting our nails with anxiety, being expedient, using means less than God's highest even to further his own work, the world does not see us trusting. It does not see us showing any kind of practical love for the God we insist is all-powerful, all-loving, all-worthy to be trusted.

A letter from a young man in the thick of bloody action in Viet Nam, scribbled by the light of a small flare at night, demonstrates the incongruity of anxiety in a woman whom I know to consider herself a sincere Christian: "I have come to dread mail-call because Mother writes so often. I know that sounds funny because all you hear back there is how much we GI's need and want mail from home. We do. That's no lie. But instead of giving me the lift I need, Mother's letters drag me down. I want to know about home, not how much she worries about me: my wet feet, my stopping a bullet, etc. A man comes to a kind of face-to-face confrontation with God here. I feel I never knew him before. If some of those busy-body church people could sit where I'm sitting right now, they'd soon drop their pretense of loving God and begin really to love him. On a night like this one (although it is quiet right now) God is all there is. And a guy doesn't think of Him with a hymn book, either, in His best suit on Sunday. He thinks of God with mud all over Him, the way I've got mud all over me tonight. Mud and some blood from two fellows who got theirs about two hours ago. Mother is the head woman on every committee in the church, and yet she's wearing me down with her worry over me. I hope you don't think I'm complaining. Maybe I am, though. I know I shouldn't be, because it has to be hard on mothers, having their sons over here. But what good does it do for her to write all that stuff to me? I'm having to trust God, why can't she?"

"I'm having to trust God, why can't she?"

In one way, I suppose it is harder on those who wait at home, not knowing. The mental anguish of mothers and wives when their men are in danger every minute is no doubt as real as the mental anguish of the men who are in the midst of the action. And yet, this

woman's lack of love for God expressed in anxiety is
only adding to her son's anguish. It troubled him so
much he bothered to write to me in the few quiet mo-
ments between attacks.

Why do I call it lack of love for God? Because
anxiety and worry go hand in hand with lack of trust,
and trust *must* spring from love. If we permit God to
love us into loving him, as he so longs to do, we will
find trust coming as a fruit of our growing love. Growing love means growing trust. In the human sense we
cannot love someone we don't know. We cannot love
someone whose nature we cannot depend upon. It is
impossible to love God if we know so little about him
that we don't know what to expect of him in our times
of crisis. And the only way we learn to trust any person is to find out everything possible about his char-
acter, his nature, his intentions toward us. If we know
someone to be trustworthy, we trust him automatically.
Trust is not a separate virtue to be whipped up and de-
veloped. It is simply the natural, inevitable by-product
of knowing God.

And since God is love, coming to know him means
coming to love him.

Does this imply that the woman whose letters are
filled with her own anxiety and worry over her son in
Viet Nam should not be anxious about him? Should
not be concerned? No. Any normal mother will carry
her burden of concern through every minute of every
hour of every day her boy is away and in danger. But
we must keep ourselves reminded that there is a fine
line between anxiety and concern. It is a very fine
line, one we don't always recognize, but it is there.
And God has no trouble telling the difference. The fine
line between anxiety and concern is always plain to

him. He also knows that anxiety is natural to the human heart, and he does not blame us or expect us to be super-human. We all slip over into anxiety. The point we make here is that anxiety paralyzes, binds. Concern sets free. Every boy away from home in the service of his country needs desperately to be reminded of our concern, our caring. This is as essential to them as food. But when the human personality is subjected to the kinds of tension those in military combat experience, their perception is honed — they can spot the difference. Sharing our anxiety with persons already under stress is utterly selfish. They will react by pushing us away, as this boy dreads his mother's letters. Anxiety tears down, weakens. Concern builds, gives strength.

There is no way for this woman to turn off her anxiety. We are not the ones who move our destructive anxiety over into the realm of concern. God does this for us, *if* we have come to trust him. If we have come to love him enough to trust our loved ones into his hands. I know of no greater way to demonstrate love for God.

It has been said that wherever a human being is trusted, he is saved. Not in the theological sense, of course. But saved from further destruction to himself. This does not mean that all human nature is to be trusted. None of it is, in the sense that we are free to trust a human being as we trust God. But trust *is* required in our human relationships. As with trusting God, all trust is based on what we know of the person in whom we place our confidence. Trust of other human beings requires balance, intelligent knowledge of their potentials *and* limitations.

With God our trust can be abandoned, utterly free. In him are no limitations, no flaws, no weaknesses. His judgment is perfect, his knowledge of us is perfect, his love is perfect. God alone is trustworthy, and we show our love for him in direct proportion to the extent of our trust in him.

> Real love must learn to relinquish
> even what is dearest to its heart —
> especially what is dearest to its heart.

Chapter 10

Loving Enough to Relinquish

NONE OF US WILL ever relinquish a thing or a person we cherish without trust. And yet if we love, we must relinquish. There is no real love without relinquishment. This we dodge like the plague. Why, if we want someone, should we even think of giving that person up? Why, after all the years of giving him her personal care through every hour of his growing life, should a mother be expected to relinquish her son to his wife? To the freedom of living his own life? Why should she relinquish her daughter? Why should she be expected to relinquish her husband in order to free him to enjoy his leisure hours now and then in his own way?

Why is it so necessary that we relinquish into the hands of God the very life of a loved one who lies near death? Why is God so hard here? Why is love so difficult? Isn't love supposed to bring joy? Happiness? Good times together?

Love *does* bring joy and happiness and good times, but this is only part of what it brings. Love brings sorrow and heartache and pain, too. "Sorrow and love flow mingled down" through the years of anyone who dares to care. And real love requires daring. This surprises us because it seems so natural, so easy to begin to love those who attract us, those who belong in some way to us. And yet anyone who bears a child or gives love to another person should weigh the cost. Love does bring joy and, on occasion, it brings happiness and good times, but there is always the possibility of loss. With every moment of joy in any human love should come the reminder that the joy can end, the loved one can die, can stop loving in return, can grow up and go away.

"But that sounds so depressing," a young woman said to me once. "Why spoil the joy of the moment by beginning to worry about some future tragedy?"

She missed the point entirely. What is suggested here is that we begin loving by beginning to face reality at the outset. This will stop some people, the timid and frail-hearted among us. We have all heard people say they will never let themselves love once — or ever again, for fear of being hurt.

What would happen to us all if God's love were this selfish? And it is selfishness, pure and simple, that causes a person to draw back in self-protection, refusing to give love to someone for fear of being hurt. This type of self-centered human being usually causes only confusion and heartache, because his love is a *taking* love and not a *giving* love. Real love concerns itself first of all with the welfare of the loved one, not the welfare of itself.

Real love gives with its hand open.

Selfish love makes a fist to strike back if it is not made to feel wanted at all times.

Real love must learn to relinquish even what is dearest to its heart — especially what is dearest to its heart. No one ever recovers from the destruction of prolonged grief until the loved one who is dead or who is dying has been relinquished. This sounds hard because it is hard. It is the hardest thing ever asked of us in this life. Some of us would find it less difficult to give up our own lives than to give up the lives of those we love. Not always, but sometimes this is probably true because if we died, we would then not be left behind to grieve. Not all, but at least part of the difficulty of relinquishment to death is the fear of grief.

"I pray every night that I will die first," an elderly lady wrote. "I know I'd never be able to live a day without my husband. So I pray God will let me die first."

I think this woman believed she was declaring the depth of her love for her husband. She was not. She was declaring the depth of her love for herself. Death, for the one who dies, is not a horrible thing. Physical death is the big entrance into whole life. If this misguided woman loved her husband as she thinks she does, she would want to spare him the grief of her going first!

God is in charge of everything that has to do with life and death, whether we realize it or not. I do not necessarily believe he wills certain deaths and not others, but he certainly permits it all, and so we limit him when we think of his being in charge of the death only. God is also in charge of the one who is left behind.

And yet, even though God is in charge of his whole world, he waits for our cooperation, for our involvement with him in the demonstration — the continuing demonstration of love. It is because he loves us that he urges us toward relinquishment. How could it be otherwise? How, if we really stop to think it through, could we imagine that when God says we are to relinquish our beloved seed into the ground of his love, he is being a hard task master? Is he asking something too difficult for our hearts to bear? No, it is because he and he alone knows what our hearts can bear that he calls for relinquishment into his hands.

Who knows and understands the redemptive purpose of God but God himself? Would God have relinquished his own Son to the brutality of Calvary if there had been a better way? Would he have *given* as he did if there had been a more creative way to rescue the human heart from itself?

> For God so loved the world that he gave his only Son, that whoever believes in him should not perish but have eternal life.

God gave in order to continue giving.

He gave his only Son so that he could go on giving life to us — eternal life. God relinquished because he knew love operates by relinquishment. Do we know better about love than God?

Is God, when he asks us to take up our crosses and follow him — when he asks us to relinquish into his hands — asking more of us than he asked of himself?

Did he determine to make it hard for us by deciding about love one day before he decided about us? Did he lay down the hard line about self-denial before he thought of the pain and hardship it could give the people he planned to create?

When we fight the princes of love as God knows them to be—when we make up our own principles and blame God for our dilemmas when our made-up principles don't work—we are, in theory, asking foolish questions like these.

No one who thinks at all (if he believes God really is as Jesus declared Him to be) could believe him to have been quixotic about his own nature. God *is* love. He didn't have to "make up" the rules and principles of love. Anymore than he had to create himself. He is the beginning. God has always been, and because he has always been, love has always been. We are not merely asked to obey the law of one facet of God's nature. Love isn't one of his attributes — *God is love*.

And because God is, he longs for us to live love so that we will *live*. Eternal life is more than a length of life. It is a quality of life. How many times have we heard that? And yet we act as though it isn't true. Eternal life for the friend of God begins now on this earth. And it is ruled by the principle of love. This is our real salvation. Salvation through Jesus Christ clearly is the open door into everlasting love. This is why we are safe in him. Being saved by entering into a personal relationship with Jesus Christ is being *saved* because there is no safe place outside of *giving love*. Only here are we able to be recreated from the *grabbing* nature of man to the giving nature of God.

Relinquishing something or someone dear to us into the hands of God is hard, but once we have tried it, healing comes and a new interest in eternal life. A new and surprising interest in eternal life because one act of love on our part swings wide the gate to the next possibility. And the next and the next and the next. The great Going On enters into us as we enter into it.

We must not confuse relinquishment with only the crisis times at the bedside of a dying loved one or the giving up of a cherished dream. Daily relinquishment of all that we love into the hands of the God of love is the only way for our love responses to grow. When we give to God what we treasure most, we are maturing in love. When we give to God, we are learning how better to love those who need us. When we give to God, we are doing the highest and best for our loved ones. A woman told me that she gives her husband to God every morning after she has kissed him good-bye. "Somehow I feel I have given him the most beautiful gift I could give because I put him into God's hands."

It is commendable for a man to build a lovely home for his wife because a woman's home is her joy. There is only one lovelier, more creative thing he could do for her than to give her a beautiful home and that is to give her to God where all beauty and all love can surround her forever.

What exactly do we mean by a man giving his wife to God? Quite simply, it means that by an act of the man's own will, he trusts his wife — her happiness, her ability to cope with sorrow, her health, the length of her life, her disposition — into God's keeping. "Whether we live or die, we are the Lord's," Paul said. Don't we have to do our own trusting of our own lives to God? Of course, we do. But in this book we are attempting to discover how to love on this earth, to discover how to learn to love so that we can make more pleasant the lives of those with whom we live and work. And if a man truly commits his wife into God's hands, he cannot — he will not be likely to try to run her life for her. And if a woman trusts God with the details of her husband's day at the office, with his decisions, with his failures and successes, she will not be likely to try to manage his affairs. There is no need for us to take over if God has already done it. There is no need for us to dominate if we have turned the reins over to God. Relinquishing our loved ones to God is a wonderful thing to do for *them* because only God understands what they are really like. Only God knows their deepest dreams. Only he knows their limitations and their capabilities. Only he knows how to keep them in check, how to keep them living up to their best, because only he knows how *not* to apply wrong pressures. Only he knows how to apply right pressures at the right time.

Relinquishing our loved ones to God means we are free not to worry about them, not to feel we have to remake their wrong decisions. It means they are in better hands than ours could ever be, no matter how deeply we love. It also means that *we are freed in the process*. We are free to be our best selves, free to get our guidance straight from God, and so be better equipped to share with those we love. If we have found the freedom from our own opinions, so that we can hear the opinions of God, those we love will always benefit. And what we share with them will have a new, balanced objectivity — unhampered by our having to force them to see things our way.

Relinquishment of itself can be only painful. Relinquishment into the hands of God can be painful at the start, but it always develops love in the atmosphere of our daily lives.

Whatever we manage to relinquish to God as a love-offering he returns to us in love . . . his love, the love that always chooses the best for us.

Loving our loved ones and our dreams enough to relinquish them into the hands of God is possible only when we have learned to expect nothing but love from God.

> When God is limited by what happens
> to be *familiar* to us,
> love in us
> is stopped dead in its tracks.

Chapter 11

Loving the Unfamiliar

LOVING ENOUGH TO INCLUDE the unfamiliar is one of the most difficult of all aims to fulfill. But if we are to make love our aim — love as it is in the heart of God — we will have to bring ourselves to the place of being willing to love the unfamiliar.

By nature, we are provincial, exclusive, happier in what we know as "our own surroundings." This is such a part of our conditioning that (unrealistic as it is) many family groups still find it irritating when a member of that family prefers the company of an "outsider." The mere incident of having been born into a certain group of human beings, related by bloodline and environment is somehow supposed to cause every member of that group to prefer every other member of that group willy-nilly. Before travel became so easy, while the family unit *was* the "world" of the individual, this was almost a necessity. On the island where I now live, in the "old days" — the plantation era — there were about twelve "main" families living up and down this strip of coastal land. They owned the plantations. The white population before the Civil War was approximately one hundred. The Negro population nearly two thousand. The family among both groups was the center of life. Even the slaves, so far as I can discover in my research for the novels I am writing, were permitted family ties. If a man and wife happened to be owned by different masters, the man was often taken by the owner each weekend to the plantation where his wife worked so they could spend the weekend together. This, of course, was not true all over the South, but here, perhaps because of the tiny size of the island, the family unit was respected fully, even among the slaves.

This is all different now simply because we have automobiles and airplanes. There are other choices beyond one's family group. Still the conditioning remains a strong influence and over and over I have heard young married couples say they would give anything *not* to have to "buck the holiday traffic" to drive "all that way home to our parents' house" for Christmas or Thanksgiving. If they didn't do it, though, frequently it would take almost until the next family holiday to get the folks back in a good humor again.

Loving the familiar — the family, the one particular church, the sorority and fraternity ties kept up through the years, blind loyalty to one political party, friendships within only one race — all of it is natural to us for one reason or another. To learn to love the unfamiliar is unnatural to the average human heart.

Just as many people still say: "Oh, I love the Negro in his place," so we love ourselves better "in our familiar place."

One is just as contradictory to the love of God as the other.

I am convinced that most Negroes, at least those whom I know well as social friends, do not necessarily long to "get into the white man's place." They are happier with each other in their own familiar surroundings, just as their white brothers are happier. This is natural. At one period in my life in Chicago I had several Japanese friends. More often than not, they visited each other and went on picnics together because they were more comfortable together.

Families who have been truly loving through the years may well have more fun together at Christmas. There is certainly nothing wrong with a family being together. Nothing wrong about a Negro preferring to attend his own church where he has always sung in the same choir. The wrong—the contradiction to God-love comes when our love *stops* at the margins of our own small provinces. The wrong comes when we have never bothered to identify with anyone personally outside our own little group. The characteristic of *un-love* enters when we erect or keep intact a wall between us and those outside our safe little boundaries.

"I really thought we'd made some new friends we could enjoy, until we found out they were pro-administration! That finished it for my husband and me."

Love crosses political lines. Love identifies with those who do not happen to hold our political persuasions.

"My colored cook and I have wonderful conversations. I can tell her things I'd never tell anyone else.

Sometimes I wish she were white so we could really see more of each other."

Love knows no color. The Negro is just as welcome at love's table as the white. The white as the Negro. In love's sight there is no virtue in being any color, any race. There is no stigma from love's point of view. Because my own tendency is to erect barricades against white persons who do not share my feeling about being social friends with Negroes, I must constantly remind myself that love recognizes no virtue in color. I am in no way superior or more loving because I have Negro friends. This could be in part the graveclothes of old rebellions against conformity, some of which I'm sure I still drag. It is, of course, partially due to my home conditioning. I was taught not to discriminate because a skin happened to be a different color from mine. And yet some of my wise Negro friends keep me reminded that it is just plain silly to say "I love Negroes." They are just like whites, and in both races are the good and the bad, the attractive and the unattractive, the honest and the dishonest, the industrious and the lazy. God does not tell us to become particularly associated with any certain race — our own or any other. He tells us to love one another as he loved us! And this includes the unfamiliar as well as the familiar.

But to love does not necessarily mean to become socially involved. It can mean that and it often does, but this is not the point. The point is that we learn to identify sufficiently with an outsider so that we can at least train ourselves to remember that here is just another human being — in more ways like us than unlike us — for whom we are to have genuine regard.

This requires effort on our part. It requires willing-ness. It requires practice. If we are *to make love our aim,* we must work at it. Love is a gift from God, but we have to work at learning to use the gift of his love just as a boy has to work and practice to balance and propel himself up and down the sidewalks on his new Christmas bicycle.

For a year now I have practiced what I understand of God-love in the areas of my own life where I know prejudice still exists. My heart snaps shut like a big lock against the people who seem to me to be cowering in bigoted cruelty beneath the hoods and cloaks of the Ku Klux Klan. I have worked on this. There are *peo-ple* under those cloaks. People for whom Jesus Christ died. People who are just as surely included in his love as I am. He has helped me see that their bigotry is based on ignorance and fear. Some of them fear the Negro because they might lose their jobs if Negroes were permitted to be employed in their shops and stores and plants. They fear what they do not know, too. In the north as well as in the south (and partic-ularly in the south, where the Negro has always been like a part of the landscape) the white man fears so-cial contact with the Negro because he does not know him outside his role as servant. None of this realiza-tion can cause me necessarily to begin to understand or like a segregationist, but it can cause me to begin to open myself to God's longing to get through to both the white supremacist *and* me with genuine *love*.

Love is, at least *becoming* my aim. It is knocking down some of my best ego-exercises in the process, too. I enjoy my prejudices, my own special, exclusive little provincialisms as much as you enjoy yours. But what we enjoy superficially is not the issue here. Love is the issue and God has more than earned the right to expect us to love.

I have not arrived at love. No one has. Realistically, perhaps, no one will during his life on this earth. But we are told to *make love our aim,* and we are given the grace and the insight to do it by the God who created our minds and who demonstrated love before us all on his cross.

Our unlove by no means ends with our prejudices against those of another race. This makes the headlines now, but it is only one bad fruit of unlove. Far more than the members of another race causes us to cloister ourselves comfortably behind *our* familiar walls.

We gang together (excluding) around our professions, too. I think it is one of the most remarkable demonstrations of God's humor that he has, through my books, thrown me into personal contact with thousands of what I always called "the club woman, housewife type." Obviously, since I am fifty years old and have neither married nor had children, and have "religiously" avoided joining women's groups, the interests of the average homemaker are outside my realm of preference for my own life. For years I felt superior because I managed to earn my own living and run my own life without the responsibilities of a husband and children. I prided myself on my personally won freedom. Don't misunderstand — I wouldn't change places with anyone on earth, but this old provincialism is so long gone that it makes me laugh now. Some of my best friends are wives with children and. husbands. I still do not belong to women's groups, but

I write for them and for years I spoke to them almost daily. We no longer exclude each other because something of God-love has entered in and the barriers that would once have existed on both sides are almost forgotten.

As a child I "looked down my nose" at all the other children whose fathers were not professional men like mine. This is perfectly normal with children. It is abnormal, immature snobbery in an adult.

"Well, yes, they go to church. But they go to the Episcopal church or the Presbyterian church or the etc. etc."

In other words, they are, I suppose, my Christian brothers and sisters, but they are *unfamiliar* to me — I can't really be sure of their spirituality since they don't go to my church.

"I must say I was amazed. I know this fellow did not have an evangelical background and yet I honestly believe he loves Jesus Christ."

A missionary said that to me once. He had gotten far enough from his familiar home base where everyone had always been sure of everyone else's "salvation" and brand of Christianity. He had met this (to him) strange Christian on the mission field, at the edge of the jungle, and it "amazed" him to discover a touch of the familiar in him. All Christians — Roman Catholic, Methodist, Presbyterian, Episcopalian, Baptist — all of them who love Christ bear some marks of family resemblance. What might happen if we actually began to hunt for those marks of resemblance instead of picking out the marks of difference?

Love would happen, and it would go on happening.

"I don't feel as though I've been to church at all when I go to my husband's church. All that ritual and the reading prayers out of a prayer book! It just seems as though I can't wait to go back to my own church where the hymns are familiar and where they don't have crosses all over the place."

"I can't possibly see how those people feel as though they've been to church at all. The songs they sing (one couldn't possibly call them hymns!) sound like Rock 'n Roll tunes and it's all so bare and bright and empty looking. And the way they chatter and gossip before the service begins is an insult to God. I feel like running back to the quiet, lovely sanctuary of my own church every time."

When God is limited by what happens to be *familiar* to us, love in us is stopped dead in its tracks. When we grow so comfortable in the surroundings which happen to be familiar to us that God is trapped in either the jig-time tempo of a "Gospel chorus" or the lofty strains of a Bach chorale, we are missing love. And God is missing the chance to love through us.

This in no way means that all Christians should worship alike. It seems to me that our extreme variation here is one of the strengths of Christianity. But if the lady who felt ill at ease because there were crosses around could open herself to what those crosses might mean to those who worshiped there, she could be surprised. As could the other lady who felt she needed the familiar, dignified, dimly lit atmosphere of her own church sanctuary in order to meet God.

God is in the high-vaulted cathedral and the flat-topped Bible Church, longing in both places to open his loved ones to his kind of love for each other and for those "outside."

We are all so different, our environments so diverse, we cannot expect ever to feel at home everywhere and with all kinds of people. God does not expect us to be particularly comfortable in unfamiliar places, with unfamiliar persons, but he does expect us to open ourselves to loving the unfamiliar. There is nothing in God's total demonstration of love as we see it in Jesus Christ that even implies *comfort*. Loving, as Christ loved, usually implies just the opposite. Real love is ready at all times for discomfort, which is the quickest way I know for us all to realize how little we know of real love.

How little we actually participate in God-love — which always cares about and includes the unfamiliar. This, unfortunately, is because we are *exclusive* by nature, and desperately need to learn the *all-inclusive* love of God.

> True responsibility can only be understood
> as one comes to understand
> something of the very balance
> that springs only from devotion
> to God himself.

Chapter 12

The Responsibility of Love

RESPONSIBLE CHRISTIANS are balanced. They neither overdo nor underdo. In fact, although we must place our willingness to act behind our love, truly responsible persons have long ago learned that before the *doing* must come the *being*.

The dictionary gives as its first definition of *being*, the word *existence*. We mean far more than mere existence here. Move on in the list of definitions and variations of meaning in the word *being* and we come upon one which says it all in one sense: *A living person.* But in the area of the responsibility of love, we must read into this phrase, *a living person*, all that life in Christ implies. At least all we know of what it implies. Jesus declared himself to *be* life: "I am the way, the truth and the life . . ." Those among us who have tried "living" with and without a conscious relationship with Christ know that by comparison, life without him can be mere existence.

And so, for Christians who know Christ to *be* life —

who have experienced, not just the high places, but the daily hour-by-hour practicality of life lived in him — *being* means quite simply: living. Living to the brim and *over* the brim of man's capacities. Not just living through the times of joy and the even rarer times of ecstasy, but living through the times of tears and heartbreak and failure. Persons who have no conscious contact with Christ *exist* through the dark hours and rightly feel that they have done well just to survive. But those who have access to God's life can *live* in the good times and the bad.

They can live and they can also keep their balance. More accurately, they can keep God's balance. Still more accurately, God keeps his balance in them if they cooperate.

We have said that responsible Christians are *balanced*.

What does the word *balance* mean?

In the sense in which we are using it, *balance* is defined as: "A state of equipoise, as between weights, different elements, or opposing forces; equilibrium, steadiness."

We move through our days being pulled from one side to another by differing weights, differing elements, opposing forces. There is nothing we can do about these forces. They are a part of the very atmosphere of man's life on earth. But if there is a fulcrum — a point of balance, we can remain steady in spite of the pulls to either side. The fulcrum, of course, is God himself.

And since God is love, the point of balance for any person, under any circumstance, is active participation in *responsible love*.

True responsibility, as I see it, can only be understood as one comes to understand something of the very balance that springs only from devotion to God. It is quite possible to fulfill one's *duties* to a cause, a denomination, an organization, to the members of one's family or social group, and still understand little of the true meaning of *responsible love*. If we are merely fulfilling our duties to a group, we first of all attempt to do what the group expects of us. If it is a religious organization, such as a church, a denominational office, a mission board, it is easy to assume that what the group requires is also the requirement of God. In some cases, of course, this is true. But we should be aware that this is not necessarily so.

Across the centuries Protestants and Roman Catholics have not acted in responsible love toward each other. Politely, perhaps piously, (although not always!) they have been "at each other's throats" in sermons, in print, in action. I can remember when an eight-year-old school friend and I avoided the subject of "going to church" because it made us feel strange with each other. She was from a Roman Catholic family and I was from a Protestant family. Neither of our mothers was responsible for this barrier between us, but children sense strangeness, differences, and so, because my school friend and I loved each other, we studiously avoided talking about what we did on Sunday mornings. When I remembered that she was a Roman Catholic, something shadowy and unfamiliar rose between us. In retrospect, I can see now that the same was true with her about me.

Try, for just a moment, to think what grief this

must have brought to the heart of God, to see strangeness between two children — both of whom attended Christian churches.

In his book, *Congo Crisis,* Joseph T. Bayly writes of the responsible love — the infinite balance that took over in the hearts of the Christian men who were imprisoned together in one small room in Stanleyville — expecting any moment, to die.

> The Congolese pastor, speaking to his fellow prisoners who were about to die, emphasized this truth: 'Roman Catholic is a name; Protestant is a name; but the One who died on the cross to save us from our sins is the Lord Jesus Christ, whom God the Father gave to redeem us. Trust Him.' Charles Davis (Missionary to the Congo under Africa Inland Mission) mentions the same fellowship of Roman Catholics and Protestants. "The last three weeks we were imprisoned, most of the other prisoners were Catholics. There was a drawing together on the basis of what people really were, (their *beings*) rather than the title they bore. Among Protestants, you found that titles such as Presbyterian, Evangelical Covenant, Baptist, etc. all fell away and you got to the core of the matter: was this person a brother in Christ? And the titles Catholic and Protestant became unimportant in those extreme days . . . It was very obvious at Hotel des Chutes and the Victoria Hotel that fellowship was on the basis of whether a person expressed Christian love or not. Paul Carlson himself said that his life was saved a half-dozen times by the love shown to him by Catholic priests along the route as he made his way to Stanleyville. Love became the important measure of faith in those days, rather than the title you bore or the religious habit you wore."

These men had been brought to the balance of responsible love toward each other by what Mr. Bayly calls "the bridge of suffering." But he also declares that

> . . . it would not be quite accurate to credit the bridge of suffering completely for this fresh, living rapport between Protestants and Roman Catholics during the Congo crisis. Without doubt, the reconciling influence of Pope John XXIII and the Vatican Councils were important factors.

God is breaking through to his loved ones with the key to love: the achievement of balance between opposing forces which alone can bring us to the place of being willing to be responsible one to another.

And God is breaking through the only way he has ever been able to break through to his stubborn children: by bringing them back to the source of love — himself.

During his last imprisonment, Dr. Paul Carlson was reading a book by Hans Kung which had been given to him by a Catholic priest on his way to Stanleyville. In *Congo Crisis* Joseph Bayly quotes one passage Dr. Carlson read and it almost perfectly describes the man who has found the balance of responsible love:

> This man is a man who will not dash off on a charger, but whose power lies in quietness and trust (Isaiah 30:15, 16), who receives the kingdom of God like a little child (Mark 10:15), and who says nothing else than a Marian "Let it be to me" (Luke 1:38); a man who expects nothing from himself, but expects all from God, who is completely open to that which is his only refuge — this man is the man who does not work but *believes,* and therefore radically excludes any self-boasting.

It is quite possible that we lose our balance, get off the track of responsible love—"dash off on a charger"

— because we *work* when we should be believing. We concentrate on *doing* when we should be concentrating on *being* and our equilibrium is tipped hopelessly to one side — is lost. We lose our balance.

What are you really like inside?

What am I really like inside?

Do we act from motives of responsible love? Do we write checks to missions and charitable causes because the very love of God has been shed abroad in our hearts? Or do we do it for some eternal reward or for income tax deductions and the approval and praise of the others who know of our gifts and write us letters of thanks and flattery?

Do we attempt to stand in the shoes of the young people in our lives because we sincerely *want* to know how it feels to be young in our time? Because we hope that somehow by our identification with them, we can come to the kind of understanding that expands and does not alienate?

Do we give our gifts at Christmas and on birthdays because we want to please the hearts of our loved ones? Or because we feel we have to do our duty by them?

More than our attitudes of heart toward other people, what is our attitude of heart toward ourselves in relation to other people? Do we visit the lonely because they are lonely or because we feel somebody should do it? Do we attempt to dispel fear because we hate the effect of fear in any human life, or do we do it because frightened people are a nuisance and the sooner they get over it the better for us?

I only know to ask these questions because I am forced often to examine my own attitude of heart. Even when I am "doing" what is expected of a Christian, I have learned the hard way that if my motives are not the motives of responsible love, they are not the motives of love at all.

Now, this is in no way intended to propagate the ancient exercise of self-deprecation, self-flagellation, self-hate. These are self-centered time wasters. You're no worse than I am and I'm no worse than you. There is no virtue involved in declaring ourselves to be the "chiefest of sinners." Virtue isn't ours anyway, it is God's. Our part is to clear out the trash scattered among our good intentions and then go on without a single backward look to permit God to teach us how to love responsibly.

The best way I know to begin is to remember that tucked into the word responsibility is the word *response*. The person who is learning to love responsibly is the person who is learning to respond — not only to those whom he finds easy to love, but to those with whom he disagrees, who naturally repel him, who have mistreated or in some way failed him. The person who is learning to respond even to strangers and difficult relatives!

A genuine response pulls something out of us toward the other person. Genuine response has to move outward; it cannot move any other direction. Outward, toward another, the way God's love moves. We flail ourselves again and again because we do not respond properly to God. This is another gigantic waste of time on our part. The only way to learn to respond adequately to God is to concentrate on *God's response to us*. God has been responding to the needs of his loved ones from the moment of creation. We ignore him much of the time, but our God is a God of the stretched-out hands. He is always offering. And it could be that the best and highest response we can ever make to him is simply to receive what he is always trying to give. I can think of no more humbling thing. No more freeing thing. The proud heart cannot receive, even from God. Therefore it cannot respond to him. We cannot learn humility. It is a gift: the inevitable result of having learned something of the nature of the responsible love of God.

In the book which Paul Carlson was reading at the time of his death, is this line also:

> In justification the sinner can give nothing which he does not receive by God's grace. He stands there with his hands entirely empty.

Is it possible that continuing knowledge of the nature of responsible love can throw more light on a seldom considered area of what man calls *justification?* If it is true, and I believe it is, that "In justification the sinner can give nothing which he does not receive by God's grace . . ." then our very ability to give love is intricately a part of our justification. God never does anything that in any way excludes the *dynamic action* of love. I have written it many times; here it is again: God is always in motion toward us, as love is always in motion toward the loved one. God doesn't busy himself with theological acts on one hand and love acts on the other. Justification by God means far more than the proverbial insurance policy toward an entrance into heaven. Any act of God is an act of *wholly responsible love*. The Christian whose main concern is his own justification has missed the point entirely. He has missed the meaning of love. Love never concerns itself with itself. Love is a continuing response *outward*.

In our relationships with other people on this earth, the two forces which pull us in opposite directions are the forces of the pull *inward,* which we motivate, and the forces of the pull *outward,* which come from God.

When we permit him to occupy the fulcrum point, balance results — and responsible love. We are not to ignore ourselves. We are to concern ourselves with the state of our *being,* and the *doing* will take care of itself. Both pulls are essential to balance. We must recognize our own needs and the needs of others. But we lose our equilibrium if God is not at the center of our living.

> The courage and daring to speak the truth
> as we see it
> are governed by our ability to love.

Chapter 13

Loving Enough to Speak the Truth

DOES SPEAKING THE TRUTH have to do with loving? Yes. In every way.

The courage and daring required to speak the truth as we see it, are governed by our ability to love. But there is a fine line of difference between speaking the truth for love's sake and insisting upon what we know of truth for the sake of proving ourselves right.

We are all familiar with the type of politician or preacher who pounds his fist and shouts as he pummels his captive audience with "his special truth." Now, shouting and pounding one's fist do not necessarily diminish truth. In the past, many of God's great men spoke truth with melodramatic gestures and clarion voices. Our great politicians and statesmen "orated" when they spoke because this was the fashion of the day. But then or now, only the dull of mind could miss sensing when a man's ego "shouted" louder than his truth.

Truth comes through loud and clear *only* when the

one who speaks it is, in his heart, *being* truth. The politician who declares from the rooftops his adherence to the Constitution of his country, but who is known to favor one group over another cannot be taken too seriously. (Wouldn't it be refreshing if a whole new school of politics sprang up in which we could be startled into voting for men who surprised us by *being* what their speeches declare? Of course, this is not good "politics." It is usually only after a man is elected and reaches the stature of *statesman* that he feels free to speak the truth as he sees it. Perhaps we should be glad for this much.)

The servants of God who live the truth and speak it with clarity get through to their listeners. But how many of us love enough to do this? How many of us have learned how to love enough to *be* truthful in our private lives? In our daily rounds? In his book, *Shantung Compound,* (Harper and Row) Langdom Gilkey, writing of his imprisonment in 1943 in a Japanese prison camp, shares what he learned of the lack of love in the hearts of some of the most theologically straitlaced among his fellow prisoners. Even ministers began to squabble about shares of food, and they did not stop with squabbling, but stole from each other. A former British soldier, an alcoholic, was virtually the only man who could be trusted to guard the food store without stealing for himself, and yet Gilkey wrote:

> Many a pious diner, whose ration of food depended on (this soldier's) strength of character, still thought of him as immoral because he drank. Some of the devout refused to lend their canteen cards to heavy smokers — but they would not hesitate for a minute to barter the packages of cigarettes they received from the Red Cross for extra supplies of food for themselves.

When their own comfort was hard-pressed, some of these Christians were unable to live truth. Langdom Gilkey quoted Brecht's sardonic couplet: " 'For even saintly folk will act like sinners, Unless they have their customary dinners.' "

Who can say how we would react under the same circumstances? One can only know that it is *possible* (because the same Christ lives in us all) to *be* truth, regardless of the circumstances and the pressures. It is impossible to speak the truth effectively unless one has first learned how to live love. Theological truths can be clarified, doctrines set out in rows, Scripture quoted at length, but *truth* is irrevocably involved with love.

Here we run head-on into the shameful fact that so few persons have the love to speak the truth. Politicians and preachers and writers flirt with truth, speak out with just enough of it to get by with their own particular constituents. If a man is in politically conservative country, he hammers away at the Federal Government for "taking us over." If he is before an audience made up of union members, he slams management; before management, he booms for big business. I wish I believed this to be an over-simplification. I do not. A few months ago two friends and I were parked beside a tiny, rural railroad station near the island where I now live, waiting to flag the northbound train. A pleasant looking, disheveled, but obviously "important" gentleman paced up and down, surrounded by a small contingent of admirers waiting for the same train. Suddenly he spotted a tag on the front of our car which told him we were residents of his county, and at almost the same moment, we recognized him as a well-known local politician.

In a flash, he was at the window of our car shaking hands *and* (because so many persons in this area are anti-Washington) began to lambast the President. We stopped him immediately. "It will simplify matters if you know, Congressman, that we admire the President. We don't know anyone else who could do the job he's doing under such difficult circumstances." He flushed momentarily, recouped, and began heartily to agree with us.

I am fully aware that it is unrealistic, but is it wrong to expect the men who represent us in Government to care enough to speak the truth? It insults my intelligence (as this man did that day) for an official to claim that he is the "Representative of all the people," when he plainly "talks one way back home" and another way in Washington.

If this sounds too naive, we can move away from politics and religion into the area of the daily life of any one of us. "How do I look in this dress?" your neighbor asks. You shudder inwardly, repelled by the fact that a woman her age would try to dress like a teenager, but you say cheerily: "Oh, I love it on you!" But do you love her? Not really. Certainly not enough to speak the truth to her. You send her out feeling attractively dressed, her ego flattered and soothed, but sure everyone else will shudder as you shuddered when you saw her tucking her middle-aged bulges into a sheath no one past the age of twenty-five should wear.

At least once a week I receive (unsolicited, you can be sure) a manuscript from someone who wants to become a published writer. Almost without exception the manuscripts are returned unread. I have no other choice because it takes time I cannot spare to read and criticize a manuscript. And, anyway, I'm certainly not an editor. But, once in a great while, I make an exception. Being a writer myself, I know how much acceptance can mean. One's own heart goes into a big stack of manuscript pages, whether the content is junk or literature. But if I really am living God-love, I am truthful with the would-be author. If I see no merit at all in it, I say so, if I am speaking the truth in love. Nothing could be more cruel than to give false hope.

Too often we think of the phrase "speaking the truth in love" as merely having to do with the tone of voice, the intent of heart. It does have to do with these, but deeper still — if we do not love, we will, nine times out of ten, not speak the truth. We will gloss it over, side-step, let them down easy — anything to avoid telling the truth.

Why do we do this? For many reasons: because we feel sorry for someone, because we are "chicken," because we won't take the chance of being disliked for having told the bare truth. But if we *love,* if we have genuine concern for the welfare of the other person, we are not afraid to be truthful. And if our motives are the motives of love, we will speak the truth in tenderness, carefully, never brusquely. Sometimes there is no other way but to hurt, if we tell the truth. This is the constant chance love takes. But real love takes it.

Of course, there are times when it is best — when it is the loving thing not to blurt out the whole truth. There are times when we need to withhold until there is more readiness to hear. This is a different thing entirely. I did not say that it is best to lie — ever. But there are situations when nothing whatever is accomplished by telling a thing, even though it is true. Sometimes the other person is just not ready to face the truth. Not ready, or too ill or weak. When my father was dying of leukemia, he was never told he had it. This seems strange to most people. We are convinced it was the right way to be with him. He had a child-like, buoyant nature, and his doctor agreed with us that his chances to survive would be lessened if he knew the hard facts. There is nothing of the nature of love in a "friend" running to a woman to tell her of her husband's latest escapade. I bring this up because *too many of us gossip under the guise of being truthful.*

What we are attempting to share in this chapter goes far deeper than mere telling the truth or lying. If we love, we simply do not lie. Jesus left us the commandment to love, and if we love, we automatically keep all the Ten Commandments of Moses. Love covers them all, including lying.

Here, we are intent upon making two main points clear: If we love enough, we will dare to speak the truth at the right time. If we do not love enough, we will be expedient — we will live by compromise.

Living by compromise is living in unlove.

If we live, compromising our own integrity in our work, in our family relationship, in our churches, we are not living love. The minister who "tones things down" so there will be "harmony" at the next official meeting is not living in love. If God has told him to speak Christ's viewpoint on a social issue, a moral issue — or both, and he skirts the edges safely, he does not love enough to speak the truth. If an author tailors his work to a particular publisher's doctrinal barriers, compromising his own beliefs in order to sell books, he does not love enough to write the truth. If he admits he is writing to sell, that's another thing and a far better thing than if he pretends he is anointed from on high to declare "truth."

One of the most potent examples of a woman who loved enough, happens to be the South's truly great writer, the late Lillian Smith. In 1944 she wrote a novel entitled *Strange Fruit*. As *Look* magazine's senior editor, George B. Leonard, wrote of her in his magnificent interview with Miss Smith, published in the September 6, 1966 issue:

> (Her novel) . . . shocked the South and made her the darling of critics who thought themselves liberal on race. Some of these critics kept expecting another *Strange Fruit,* and when it did not come (her spirit grew; her writing encompassed not just race but all of humankind), they simply interpreted each new book in terms of their earlier favorite. To them, Lillian Smith would always be "that little lady in Georgia who wants to help the Negroes," and nothing more.

The rigid Southerner went on fearing her, resenting her. More than resenting, certain of her neighbors burned her home, destroying all her letters, her mementos, her manuscripts and pictures.

Neither those who began to minimize her nor those who persecuted her could silence Miss Smith's truth. She loved them both enough to speak out and to go on speaking out through her thirteen years during which she was a victim of terminal cancer. She died in a hospital in Atlanta, as I wrote this chapter. But her writings are still speaking the truth in love. She was not, as her enemies declared, a "nigger-lover." She was a lover of mankind. This woman cared about us all, black and white and yellow, as few human beings have ever cared — enough to tell the truth as she saw it without compromise.

Those who remain great in the history of any land, loved enough to speak the truth, to live truth, even when it challenged their popularity. At a time when the word "Union" was despised, Lincoln, in his second Inaugural Address said:

> With malice toward none; with charity for all; with firmness in the right, as God gives us to see the right, let us strive on to finish the work we are in; to bind up the nation's wounds.

In a letter to a friend in 1816, Thomas Jefferson, from a heart troubled by the controversy over our Constitution which still rages today, dared to write:

> Some men look at constitutions with sanctimonious reverence, and deem them like the ark of the covenant, too sacred to be touched . . . Laws and institutions must go hand in hand with the progress of the human mind. . . .

Paul and Peter and thousands of followers of Jesus Christ went gladly to their deaths because they chose to love enough to speak the truth and not to compromise.

Jesus himself was crucified because he would not, could not compromise what he knew truth to be. Every moment of his earthly life, he lived truth because he was truth. "I am the way, the truth and the life," Jesus declared. This was madness to those who lived bound by the rigidities of the "popular" religious concepts of his time. More than madness, his words were considered blasphemy. But the fact remained: He *was* the truth and the life, and so he spoke and so he lived. And because he did, so he died, leaving behind him men and women whom Paul described as being under the control of the *love* of Christ. "For the love of Christ controls us." And so they lived "no longer for themselves but for *him* who for their sake died and was raised."

If we live truth, as Lillian Smith lived truth, as the Christian martyrs lived truth, we live Christ, and the same power that raised him from the dead will give us the courage and the daring to love enough to speak the truth.

We cannot all see all of truth, cannot all see all of what is wholly right, but we can "with firmness in the right, as God gives us to see the right," learn to love enough to demonstrate in our words and in our lives what we do see.

> . . . we cannot learn to demonstrate love
> to others until we have learned
> how to love ourselves.

Chapter 14

Loving Ourselves

THIS MAY COME AS a surprise to some, but it is impossible to learn to love others enough until we have learned how to love ourselves — rightly.

There is a kind of spiritual masochism which runs like an odd thread through the writings of many of the ancients and, unfortunately, it is still running through some of today's writing. This thread of self-deprecation is certainly not there without reason. But here, perhaps as much as in any other area of Christian thought, it seems to me we have been one-sided — out of balance. At the heart of the Christian message (from our side) is the need for repentance, the recognition of the helplessness of man to change his own nature. This has been made abundantly clear. Anyone who has glimpsed the truth of the cross of Christ has had to see his own need of a Saviour. Otherwise, the cross has only sentimental meaning. As a human being approaches Christ, his seeing is sharpened in two directions at once: He is enabled to see

his own sinfulness *and* the love of God simultaneously.
One without the other would be futile. God, of course,
knows this, and so he gives us this necessary double
vision.

But the human tendency to splinter off into divi-
sions, into "groups," tend to grab one revelation or
the other, seldom both. One faction emphasizes only
the sinfulness of man, another only the love of God.
Those who dwell only on the love of God become overly
permissive. They preach and practice what can be destructive license. Those who dwell only on the sinfulness of man become overly-strict, rigid, egotistical.
They are so busy running down their imagined
"selves" that their healthy selves fight back. And when
the God-made self fights back instead of entering into
God-love, as it was created to do, it grows abnormally.
Have you ever noticed that the most rigid Christian,
the one who makes a special point of his fundamental-
ism and his salvation (consciously or unconsciously)
frequently possesses an outsized ego? An ego that
forces the rest of us to tread softly around it for fear
of antagonizing? This is frequently the person who
bears down on the sinfulness of man, on man's de-
pravity, his total unworthiness — who seems to glory
in discussing his spiritual battles, his black heart and
of course, the black heart of others. The normal ego
is squeezed down so that it bulges out in an abnormal
direction. Like an ugly growth on a person's face, it
ends up calling attention to itself. Over-depreciation
of the self is every bit as egoistic as vanity. It is in
reality, a kind of vanity.

The persons who seem to ignore the sinfulness of
man, (a condition which produces an equally one-sided
state,) tend, of course, to go to the other extreme. Its

adherents appear to love themselves, but they are in fact equally as unself-loving as the first group. The end results are also abnormal distortion of the human self, because man cannot love himself rightly until he has seen his self in need of a Saviour.

Balanced, true self-love — the kind Jesus mentioned as normal, comes only when our sight of the cross is remembered and practiced in the round: When we see both our own sinfulness *and* the love of God.

This is perhaps a suitable time for me to share what I believe to be deeper *seeing* on my part through the years which have passed since I wrote a book titled: *Early Will I Seek Thee.* (Fleming H. Revell, 1956) In that book, I was "lit up" with my first glimpse into the vital truth contained in Galatians 2:20:

> I have been crucified with Christ; it is no longer I who live, but Christ who lives in me; and the life I now live in the flesh I live by faith in the Son of God, who loved me and gave himself for me.

This is still an important truth to me. I believe it more fully, if anything, than I did during the writing of the earlier book. But the clarification which has come with the years has to do with the unhealthiness of attempting to "kill off the self." This is not only unsound, it is impossible. And the attempt to do it can lead to abnormality in the human personality. I can only be thankful that God has never permitted me for long to become "hung up" on one verse, or one doctrinal slant. Daily life with the person of Jesus Christ should bring continuity, wholeness — not division and special emphasis. Consequently, I regret that I am still receiving an occasional letter from some overly-impressionable reader who, because of one somewhat over-simplified chapter in my book, *Early Will I Seek Thee,* is still attempting suicide of the self. Even then I saw that this is not possible. We *have been* crucified with Christ. We do not engineer the crucifixion. And yet troubled people or unthinking people grasp at half of this truth and damage themselves on it. To concentrate on denegating the self is in-going, not out-going, and therefore is not love.

As I see it now, the self-centered "self" was crucified with Christ. That is, the helplessness of the human nature against sin was remedied. Help has come in Christ. We need no longer repeat our sins, our misdeeds. We need no longer carry around our personality twists, our pet indulgences. We can, but we don't need to now that we have identified with his death and resurrection. Redemption is God's plan to *restore* our selfhood as he originally planned it, not kill it off.

But a careful look back through Christian literature shows that man's tendency to run himself down has often taken over. We had better begin to concentrate on *balance,* because if any people on earth have access to balance it is the people of God.

There is no denying the sinfulness of man, but there is also no denying his value to God. Here again, there is a rest-producing balance, if we will only stop to think about it: Because man needed a Saviour, Jesus died, *and* because man had worth to God, Jesus died.

Why do we stop with one side or the other? Why is it so easy for the human personality to lean toward imbalance?

When Jesus told us that we were to love our neighbors as ourselves, He was assuming man's love for himself. And I do not believe Christ was assuming the wrong kind of self-love. If he had been, he would not have instructed us to love our neighbors with that kind of love! He simply *had* to be assuming the potential in man of learning to love himself in a balanced way, rightly, normally. Nothing is required really, except the willingness to take a little time to think through what he said.

And it is needful to repeat that we cannot learn to demonstrate love to others until we have learned how to love ourselves. If Christ does live in us now, anyone can learn how to love himself with the same God-love with which Christ loves. And the love of God for man concerns itself with man's balance, his openness, his healing from the sins of distortion, his creativity. God-love is always creative love. He is the Creator. God's love is always redemptive love. He is the Redeemer. Within the human limitation, our love can demonstrate the same qualities.

We decide.

Now, what are some of the barriers to our learning to love ourselves as God means us to love?

One barrier is, I believe, wrong conditioning. Somewhere along the line, we have gotten hold of the idea that self-love is wrong, is sinful. The salvation of God is somehow supposed to snuff out the self. If this were true, do you suppose God would have gone to the lengths he did to redeem us? We are not to stop loving our selves, *we are to begin*. It is not possible to love one's self in the sense of God-love until one has become a Christian. The most balanced, intelligent men and women I know who are not believers, will show, sooner or later, a streak of self-hate. Only God can change this. We go on letting ourselves down, we go on failing and fumbling, but only those who know what to do with their failures and fumbles can avoid self-hate. Hate is the opposite of love, and if God is love, then hate is the opposite of God. The rare human being who has learned how to love himself, can receive a compliment or a criticism with equilibrium — without the end result of either self-hate or self-adoration.

Another block to right self-love is our blindness to what it really is. The love of God never pampers. Self-love in the light of Christ cannot possibly mean self-indulgence. We tend to equate self-love with self-indulgence and this is a desecration of the true meaning of the word *love*. We should have love's meaning clear: God-love which concerns itself wholly for the loved one; God-love which demands our best and offers grace for our second best.

Perhaps one of the most misleading phrases we use in relation to God is to say or think that this or that "is pleasing" to him. This immediately puts him in the unnatural, unrealistic position of a person whose pleasure we have to court, to woo. Nothing could be further from the truth. God knows as no one else knows, that we satisfy his heart in the highest sense when we learn to love him enough to love ourselves, and then to love others.

I am now in the difficult, but determined process of learning to love someone whom I do not like at all. I don't trust him, I find him boring, shallow, cruel at times. Some of his "christian" ethics move me close to righteous indignation (if human beings are capable of that reaction — a thing about which I am not yet certain.) But God has told me during the writing of this book that I am to begin to share his concern for this man as a fellow human being whether he behaves as a Christian brother or not. Who knows? I may end up rather liking him too, but this is not required.

Many of us cannot like ourselves, but if we begin to love ourselves with God-love, we may end up liking ourselves. If we recognize that in order to love, we need not necessarily like, (prefer), we have eliminated another barrier to healthy self-love.

Still one more obstacle to genuine concern for our selves will vanish when we begin to realize the truth behind the statement that we *cannot* learn to love others until we have learned to love ourselves. First of all, if we do not love ourselves it will be difficult for us to believe that anyone else would want our love. God handled this unnecessary twist on the cross, if we will only look at him there. He was there for us, too, and if God (the supreme lover) cared enough about us to endure the cross for love of us, isn't our love worth something to another human being? If this sounds vague, too theological, remote — try it. The principle of practice applies here: Even if you don't feel your love is important, give it anyway. Any act of ours undertaken in faith in God is his responsibility. This is one of the most stimulating ways to learn of God's sense of responsibility toward us — acting on something for his sake and leaving the results to him. The results or the consequences. If things turn out badly, he can handle that too.

We must think now about the effect on the *object* of our love when we love ourselves enough. I know of no better way to swing our perspectives into focus where the necessity for the right kind of self-love is concerned. An example: If you love your wife or your husband or your friend or your child, you will only be able to contact them with that love *if* you are loving yourself — are showing practical concern for your own well being. For example, we are *not* loving someone else enough if we do not take care of our physical as well as our mental and spiritual health. If we overeat or overindulge in any way — if we fail to get proper exercise, we are possibly shortening our life on earth. We are showing lack of concern, utter lack of love for those who love and depend on us. I suppose I will struggle to my grave with the problem of overweight, but I can show my love for those who love me by controlling it. Remaining overweight is proof that I am unable to love my loved ones enough because I do not love myself enough.

This kind of unlove is not limited to the physical. If you are an habitual gossip, you do not love enough. Not only do you not love the object of your gossiping, you do not love yourself nor the members of your family enough either. Gossip distorts us, pulls us into abnormal avenues of thought and heart and this has to show up in our daily lives whether we're gossiping at the moment or not. Gossip disintegrates the gossiper, destroys him as well as others.

There is still another barrier to the right kind of self-love: We simply do not believe thoroughly in the redemptive power of Jesus Christ. We do not need to prefer ourselves in order to love anymore than we need to like ourselves. *But we do need to recognize our own individual potentials in God.* When we fail to do this, we are failing to participate in his continuing redemption in us. Dr. E. Stanley Jones once said to me: "Now, you are neither worm nor wonder, but a bundle of possibilities in Jesus Christ." I have never forgotten his words. I hope I never will. This truth makes it simpler to live with myself in a balanced, healthy, creative way. It keeps my self in its proper place in my own regard and in the regard of God.

Jesus assumed a right kind of self-love first when he said we were to love our neighbors as ourselves. And in his words I find my certainty for believing that it will be forever impossible for us to love our neighbors, our friends, our families or our enemies, until we learn, by grace, and through the infinite balance and patience of God, to love ourselves.

> . . . we can all learn to love
> enough to laugh —
> even with those who don't agree
> with us.

Chapter 15

Loving Enough to Laugh

THAT "A MERRY HEART doeth good like a medicine," no one can doubt. But we think too seldom of merriment, light-heartedness, cheer as being integral parts of love. We think too seldom of the fact that we can cultivate cheerfulness, good humor, even joy in the practice of love.

Cultivate it? Yes. All of learning to love involves our will to love. As we have said, there is no hypocrisy here. When we are about the Father's business of loving, we are in his will, and when we act in God's will regardless of how we feel about it, we are not being hypocritical. We are being Christian.

Some of us are inclined to moroseness by nature, but this does not mean we need to give in to it. It merely means that we will need to use a bit more will power in order to learn to cultivate the tendency to cheerfulness. We err when we call a naturally cheerful person "more spiritual" than persons inclined the other way, but the people who find it easy to laugh and those

who find it difficult, need to delve beneath the surface
of laughter and find its relationship to love.

It has been rightly said that *sanity* is the state of
taking the right things seriously and that *insanity* is
taking the wrong things seriously. By the same token,
the sane, balanced, mature individual takes the right
things lightly. Just as the off-balance person takes the
wrong things lightly.

Our laughter tells more about us than we think. The
person whose laughter crackles through at the "wrong"
time creates tensions, irritates, makes for awkward
situations. The sardonic laughter that frequently goes
along with cynicism, sarcasm and gossip hurts feelings. It can even cause heartbreak — certainly embar-
rassment. Silly, self-conscious laughter at what appears to be nothing, not only bores, it exposes super-
ficiality or tensions in the one who indulges in it.

But wholehearted, ready laughter heals, encour-
ages, relaxes anyone within hearing distance. The
laughter that springs from love makes wide the space
around it — gives room for the loved one to enter in.
Real laughter welcomes, and never shuts out. But if
we attempt merely to learn when and when not to
laugh, how and how not to sound when we laugh, we
will end up with nothing. Real laughter goes all the
way *in* to love. Real laughter requires relaxation and
the tensions go.

The parent, who laughs *at* the awkwardness of a
child, can mark that child permanently, can make him
feel unloved. Perhaps nothing of an ordinary nature
can hurt more or bless more than laughter. We need
to give our laughter some personal attention.

If we love, we will not laugh at the wrong times. If we love, we will not withhold laughter when it is needed. And perhaps we should begin by checking our abilities to laugh rightly at ourselves. This, of course, is one of the big signs of a balanced personality: the ability to laugh at oneself. A friend of mine, whose spiritual perception about other people is excellent and who always sees the holy hilarity potential in someone else's predicament, simply has no humor at all about herself. This would seem to be a contradiction, but I wonder if it is as unusual as it appears on the surface.

Most of us, I fear, fail to see anything funny in our own predicaments. And sometimes there is nothing funny. Which brings us to face the fact that laughter, genuine laughter, does not have to be motivated by something that simply strikes us as humorous. Authentic laughter doesn't even need to make a sound. The source of real laughter is inner-balance and love. We only know when and when not to laugh according to our innersensitivity to others and to ourselves.

We tend to avoid the deadly serious person when possible, don't we? Why is this? It can be for no other reason than that God created us in need of joy and merriment. "A merry heart doeth good like a medicine." It does. The word *merry* implies "pleasant, delightful, uninhibited joy and frolic, festivity." And I see nothing whatever in the Bible that indicates that God is against merriment. Not only did the writer of the proverbs declare that "a merry heart doeth good," Jesus himself in his magnificent story of the prodigal son, showed unmistakably that God is in favor of festivity. In this parable, as in every word and act of his

life among us, Jesus was telling and showing us what
the Father is really like. His mission on earth was to
declare the true nature of God. The father in the story
of the prodigal son showed to both his sons — the was-
trel prodigal and the faithful, but self-righteous elder
son — a love *like* the love of God. And when the prodigal came home repentant, his father welcomed him,
as God welcomes us, with joy and merriment. He threw
an enormous party!

> . . . the father said to his servants, 'Bring quickly the
> best robe, and put it on him; and put a ring on his hand,
> and shoes on his feet; and bring the fatted calf and kill
> it, and let us eat and make merry; for this my son was
> dead, and is alive again; he was lost and is found.' And
> they began to make merry.

There was music and there was dancing and there was
feasting — all because of the joy in the father's heart.

Christians who think they are glorifying God by
wearing long faces and letting the laughter and fun
die out of their lives, choked by a wad of prohibitions,
are disagreeing with Jesus in his own estimate of the
Father he came to declare.

There is a decided difference between authentic joy
and false merriment. Most of us know false merriment. Some of us have worked at it in our own lives,
have heard the brittle rasp of false, critical laughter,
have participated in the hollow attempt man makes at
enjoying himself by trying to whip up joy and merriment through various excesses. This does not work,
except to destruction. And yet, no one who knows
Jesus Christ has any right whatever to condemn those
who seek so desperately for makeshift happiness, for
makeshift joy. God created the need for genuine happi-

ness in every human being. It is only natural for people who have not found joy first hand in Christ to
"knock themselves out" hunting it elsewhere. The
Christian should be the last to condemn and the first
to understand the mad, determined search of the pagan
mind. Joy and happiness and merriment blot out pain
in the heart, dim mental suffering. Most people who
indulge in excesses are hunting for blotted out pain
and dimmed suffering. They are hunting for joy and
merriment and real laughter. To condemn them for the
search is to miss the point of God's love. Instead of
condemning with a long face, from a do-it-yourself
pedestal of "spirituality" (as false as their "merriment"), we should learn to love them enough to begin
to share the joy we know in living with a conscious-
ness of God.

Where appropriate, we can all learn to love enough
to laugh — even with those who don't agree with us.
There is no better place to begin practicing this kind
of love than the next political or religious argument
that comes along. Hackles never rise higher than when
a conservative and a liberal Christian or voter "go at
each other" over their pet theories. But if only one person in the room backs off just long enough to remember that Christ died for both liberals and conserva-
tives, a love-filled objectivity can take over and laughter can result. The tensions fall away, and harmony
settles in the hearts, if not in the opinions of the
arguers.

A woman is dying a painful, slow death today from
cancer, but her humor has not been attacked by it. "It's
hard enough on my family to watch my body die. The
least I can do is show them the essential me has not
changed!"

"It was our twentieth anniversary last week and I had decided by noon that even if my husband had forgotten it, he was going to be reminded by me and we were going out for a big, expensive dinner. When he came in the front door that night, I was dressed fit to kill. He had not only forgotten our anniversary, he handed me his first paycheck on the new job and for the first time the salary cut I knew he had to take dawned on me in a practical way. I stayed dressed up. He got into a dinner jacket and we had stacks of pancakes in the kitchen and laughed together until after midnight."

She loved him enough for laughter at a predicament that could and does cause many women to dig themselves a cozy grave of self-pity.

Of course, it is totally unchristian ever to laugh *at* anyone, no matter what has happened. We all do this, even the most sincere among us. But there are times, more times than we seem to realize, when certain people in our lives must be laughed *about*. There is just nothing else to do. We all have a few persons to contend with who are so cantankerous, so difficult, so full of barbs, they leave us only two alternatives: to begin to hate them or to laugh about them. Now, in cases like these, hating is easier by far — at the moment. If not hate, then resentment. In fact, resentment requires no effort at all on our part. Effort *is* required to resist it. And I know of no better way than to laugh, whether we feel like laughing or not. Again, the principle of *acting* on what we know to be right, regardless of how we feel is the only way. And it is all involved in learning to love. Not learning to *like,* or *prefer,* but to *love.*

Anyone who is hard to take in our lives *needs* love. There is something twisted in him, something sick needing healing. "Oh, he isn't sick, he's just mean!" Sin is sickness, and only the Great Physician can heal it. And the way he has chosen to go on healing is through our willingness to love. Only when we are open to the wideness of God's own love can he heal those who are so difficult.

It would be unrealistic to insist that all of these rough-edged persons are going to be healed, made whole and become simpler for us to live with and work with. There is no guarantee of total victory. Our part is to be willing to learn to love enough not only to leave the actual results of the potential healing to God, but to learn to laugh the poison of our resentments out of own own veins.

"Sometimes I don't see how my husband stands it a day longer. The owner of his company grows more vindictive, more downright deceitful every day of his life. He tells my husband one thing and the sales manager another, as though actually trying to get them at each other's throats! But all I know to do is keep the sense of humor God gave me. I try even harder to fix dinners that please my poor, harassed husband — try to have funny things to tell him every night. After he's home for an hour or so, he's usually laughing. Only God can keep him steady, but at least I can love him enough to create a happy atmosphere for God to work in."

Loving enough to laugh at the right times, for the right reasons, knowing that God backs up this kind of love, is living in the will of the Father — is Kingdom activity that can count for all time and right on into eternity.

> God's love is utterly patient
> because God knows
> where everyone is
> on his earthly journey.

Chapter 16

For God So Loved the World

FOR GOD SO LOVED the world that he gave his only Son, that whoever believes in him should not perish but have eternal life."

Everything contained in this book — or any book on the dynamic of learning to love — is only half-truth, until these "twenty-four most important words in history" are known and acted upon, and at least in part, understood. I doubt that anyone has ever fully understood their meaning, but it is no new thing for us to dare to act upon a truth which we do not wholly understand. Science is "out of bounds" for most of us where our understanding is concerned, but we act upon its discoveries through every hour of every day. I don't even understand the mechanics of this typewriter which I use now and yet it is an integral part of my daily life. I simply pound the keys with the tips of my fingers, acting on what I *believe* will happen. Black letters form themselves into words on the page without my giving a thought to how they get there. I am left free to think

only about the words themselves, because I *believe* they
are going to appear.

We are left *free* to love as God loves when we begin
to *believe* that he revealed himself fully in Jesus Christ :
that his love can be measured by the Man on the cross.
The typewriter repair man understands how my ma-
chine works, but I don't have to. Theologians may
possess an intellectual understanding of John 3 :16 beyond what the rest of us possess, but here the analogy
breaks down. Each of us has a spiritual capacity, and
this spiritual capacity, if it is under the control of Jesus
Christ, can experience the results of truth *without* de-
tailed understanding.

God did not do what he did in Christ for a select few.
This was the wall into which Jesus crashed as he at-
tempted to demonstrate the truth about God to the
learned Jews of his day. They predicated man's salvation on how completely he had mastered the laws
and tenets of the Scriptures. This excluded the ignorant man on the street and his even more ignorant
wife at home. Jesus came declaring that his Father
loved the whole world — not just the educated few —
and they killed him for daring to say it. From their
exclusive viewpoint, he spoke blasphemy when he pinpointed this revolutionary truth about himself :

> You search the scriptures, because you think that in
> them you have eternal life ; and it is they that bear wit-
> ness to me ; yet you refuse to come to me that you may
> have eternal life.

Jesus not only came bearing revolutionary truth
about himself, he bore revolutionary truth about the
love of God — and as he bore it, he demonstrated it in
his own person, before, during, and after his crucifixion.

He was explicit at all times where his own identity and the love of God were concerned. And yet this was too much for the trained intellects of his enemies. This in no way means that the ignorant person grasps spiritual truth more easily than the educated person. It merely means that if the educated person is measuring truth by his intellect — and not his intellect by truth — he has more trouble believing simply, as a child believes. Nicodemus was an intellectually astute member of the Sanhedrin, but he did not permit his intellectual accomplishments to block his exercises of simple faith in this Man who said everything he offered hinged on *believing* in him.

Many persons profess to believe in Jesus Christ. Few seem willing to act upon that belief. They leave it comfortably stored in the realm of their minds. They have accepted a formula, a creed, not a Person. If we believe something with our whole being, *we act on it*. The follower of Christ who does not at least make an attempt to act in love toward every other human being on earth is not acting on what he claims to believe. This is not judging him in the sense of where he is apt to spend eternity. I see a conclusion like that simply as a statement of fact. Jesus instructed us to love one another as the Father loved him! We are to love the Lord our God with all our minds and hearts and our neighbor as ourselves. I see no evidence in his Commandment that authentic Christianity ever omits the act of love. Not the *feeling* of love, but the *act* of love. If we are to love one another as the Father loved Jesus, this means that we are to be willing, if the need arises, to act in love toward everyone and anyone in the world. Only God could act toward the entire world at once, but any member of the human race whose path crosses ours is entitled to our love *if* we truly believe in Jesus Christ. Regardless of what this person does to us, we are to love him. If we happen to dislike him with every fibre of our beings, if he has mistreated us, failed us, cheated us — no matter. All of this happened to Christ, but he went on loving because he could not deny the nature of love itself. He and the Father were one — Jesus was God in the flesh of man, and *God is love*.

I can't possibly imagine that Jesus of Nazareth found his enemies easy to *like*. He was tempted as we are tempted — in all the ways we are tempted. He *had* to be tempted to unlove too, because with his mind and his spiritual and mental perception, he must have found many persons dull, uninteresting, and surely he encountered extreme cruelty and betrayal and deceit and manipulation. I'm sure Jesus found it simple to dislike many people, but he also found it possible, because of his very nature, to love even those he may have disliked. In fact, God's love seems to be poured out in still greater measure toward the unlovely, the unlovable. Their need is so great. No one needs love more than the repulsive, the difficult, the disagreeable person. And if the very love of God *has* been shed abroad in the Christian's heart, he too, must free it — must let it flow in even greater measure toward that person who is "impossible to take." God, walking our earth in Jesus, did not dwell on what he had to "take." He dwelled on what he had to *give*. And by God's very nature, *he had to give*.

"For God so loved the world that he *gave* . . ."

How do we really learn to give love?

We have already said in Chapter 7 that we learn to love by loving — by being willing to act on what we know of God-love regardless of the way we feel. And there is no other way to learn the true nature of God-love aside from learning all we can learn of the true nature of God. This is only possible as we learn of his Son, Jesus Christ, who came to reveal him to us in terms we can understand — to show us, by the actions of his own earthly life lived out in circumstances like our own, how to give God-love.

We cannot, of course, whip up love on our own. And important as it is to know the principles of Christian love, I fail to see how we can merely imitate Christ in our own strength. But anyone can *live love* if the very life of God himself, in the person of his Holy Spirit, is acting in us and through us. God so loved us all that he gave his Son, Jesus, to live and die and rise again among us, but he is still *giving* now in the presence of his Holy Spirit within us. When the Christian declares that he simply can't show love to a particularly annoying human being, he is in reality declaring his refusal to cooperate with the very love of God in him! "For God so loved the *world* . . ." And that includes that person who is the seemingly eternal thorn in your flesh, in my flesh.

The giving of God-love is always possible, because as Jesus said: "With God all things are possible." We do not admit our own weakness when we fail to love, we simply admit our own stubborn refusal to permit God to be himself in us.

We've all heard people say, "If I act a way I don't feel toward him, I'll feel like a hypocrite." Nonsense. God never instructs according to our feelings about anything. ". . . that whoever *believes* in him . . ." That is God's only requirement for the showing of love to the whole world. "The love of Christ controls us," Paul

wrote. And certainly no one can say that Paul, when
his name was Saul, was by nature a loving person. In
fact, he had trouble in his human relationships most
of his life, but he had found the open secret and he
usually ended up by making use of it. Don't forget, it
was also Paul who wrote that "the love of God has
been shed abroad in our hearts." God's own love is
there to use, and his love is never, never discrimina-
tory, never exclusive, never turned inward, always
moving outward. And God's love is never given according to worth, it is always given according to the
very nature and heart of the God who is love.

At first, to act in love toward someone we dislike,
toward someone for whom we have no respect, toward
someone who has injured us, seems the hardest thing
God could ever ask. But once we have tried it, we find
that God's way is, in the long run, the more restful
way. This is only one of the ways in which he gives his
people rest. "Come unto me," Jesus said, "and I will
rest you." He will. The other person may not change
overnight, or ever, but the burden of rebellion in our
own hearts which has so tired us will lighten if we begin to act on what we truly believe about Jesus Christ.

"He's so arrogant anyway about his two hundred
dollar suits, I'm not going to flatter him by compli-
menting him. Flattery isn't Christian."

No, it isn't. But the Holy Spirit within can tell us
when our compliments edge over into flattery. If a
man's vanity over his two hundred dollar suits is that
important to him, he must be very insecure inside, and
perhaps the only door to his heart might be an honest
appraisal of his suit! After all, almost any suit that

costs two hundred dollars is at least made of beautiful material. There is nothing hypocritical about mentioning it to the wearer. Love always hunts for even the smallest chink in the armor of the needy. Love never gives up seeking out the small aperture where it can enter and bless and begin its life-transforming occupation.

Now, if none of this helps you break down your own resistance toward that person who is so hard to take, try *gratitude*. What about the circumstances of your own life? Is your health good? Can you see well? How about your hearing? Are you taking sunsets and music for granted? Have you good friends? Even one? Do you spend your days with the person you love? Or even if that person is no longer with you, did you have a good life together? Did your parents do anything for you? Are you in the work you love? Are your needs met? You aren't hungry, are you? Or penniless?

Gratitude permeated Jesus' life on earth. "Father, I thank thee that thou hast heard me."

Gratitude pries us loose from our unloving responses more quickly than anything else. None of us gives thanks enough to be good at it, but one small grateful response to God can open the door of our stubborn hearts wide enough for his love to flow out.

Most of our unloving responses are due to lack of gratitude or to impatience. God's love is utterly patient because God knows where everyone is on his earthly journey. Not only does God know where we are, he knows what we are like. Because he knows that no response, however pious it may seem to be, is an authentic love-response until we have put our wills behind it — until we have chosen it freely. He never pushes. He is patient because he knows nothing else works. He is patient because he *loves*. The best check of our love responses is a check of our *patience*. Impatience is lack of love. And God always waits for us to learn at our own learning speed, never at his. We expect others to learn at our speed, not at theirs. As my friend, Anna Mow says: "We learn faster if we are honest, but God is realistic about our learning speed."

A check of our tendency toward *arrogant judging* is a check of our ability to love. Anyone, who has glimpsed the heart of God and the hearts of the arrogant little men who stood jeering at the foot of his cross, easily despises those who judge from the viewpoint of arrogance. But it is very simple for us who see the sin of arrogant judging to slip over into it too! We can see it in someone else and begin to judge him *as he judges*.

Arrogant judging, impatience, despising for any reason are all the expressions of *unlove*. There is no mark of the eternal in them. There is no mark of belief in Jesus Christ in them. Eternal life — the particular quality of God-life offered by Jesus Christ — comes only to those who are willing to let God love the world through them. Eternal life in all its fullness comes only to those who believe in God's gift to us, his Son, Jesus. But our belief must far exceed an intellectual acceptance. The kind of faith in God that makes it possible for us to progress toward the goal of love is the faith that is willing to act in love when there is a need for love. And the first sign of trouble or disharmony anywhere is the sign that someone had better start acting in love, whether he feels like it or not. We find it much easier to love when things go well. This is not what motivated God to give his Son. The world was in trouble because the people who lived in it needed to be saved somehow from their sins.

Sacrifice is not needed when things run along smoothly. Sacrifice is needed when there is trouble, friction, want, lack of peace. When we are willing to make love our aim only when it pleases us, or at least when nothing too much is required of us, we are not loving with God-love. We have missed the dynamic urgency at the very heart of the Father. His love is poured out where the need is, which is why he pours out love toward us all every minute. We are doing no special favor when we give God's love to someone who is in the wrong. We are not acting from a pinnacle of spiritual achievement. We are merely acting in love-response to the God who gave love in his Son, Jesus . . . who still gives it, and who will go on giving it for all eternity because we will always need it. And because *God is love.*